The Effective Management of Technology

A Challenge for Corporations

Sushil K. Bhalla

BATTELLE PRESS

Columbus • Richland

Distributed by

ADDISON-WESLEY PUBLISHING COMPANY, INC.
Reading, Massachusetts   Menlo Park, California
Don Mills, Ontario   Wokingham, England   Amsterdam   Bonn
Sydney   Singapore   Tokyo   Madrid   Bogotá
Santiago   San Juan

Distributed by

ADDISON-WESLEY PUBLISHING COMPANY
Reading, Massachusetts 01867
(617) 944-3700

Library of Congress Cataloging-in-Publication Data

Bhalla, Sushil K.
  The effective management of technology.

  Includes index.
  1. Technological innovations—Management.
  2. Strategic planning. I. Title.
HD45.B47   1987   658.5   86-25847
ISBN 0-201-10929-8

Printed in United States of America

For Michelle

CONTENTS

ACKNOWLEDGMENTS

The practical utility of any creative work is limited unless it has been put to practice, in this case, the publication of this book. It would have been impossible to complete it without the tremendous support provided by my colleagues within FMC, particularly Gary E. Wolfe who has been most valuable as a reviewer and critic, Charles A. Gray for his timely and active support, Mark E. Koznarek for his active involvement in the early phases, and Lyle L. Nehls for his review, comments, and providing an opportunity to implement the concepts developed.

My association with Gary S. Stacey of Battelle Memorial Institute, played a major part in enhancing the scope of this book. I would also like to thank a number of reviewers who provided helpful suggestions and comments at different stages of writing this book, particularly Wendell J. Harkleroad of Church and Dwight Company, Robert H. Hayes of Harvard, James D. Hlavacek of the Corporate Development Institute, John M. Kucharski of EG&G, Inc., Nathan D. Lee, Consultant to FMC, and William B. Tuemmler of Pennwalt Corporation.

My gratitude to Carol A. Benci and Mary M. Lutz for assisting in the preparation of the manuscript and for their patience and efforts to keep me on schedule.

I would like to thank FMC Corporation for providing the environment that permitted me to complete this book.

This acknowledgement would be incomplete without recognizing the work of a number of people that was used throughout this book in developing and integrating different concepts for the planning and management of technology. My sincere thanks to Joseph E. Sheldrick of Battelle Press who brought it all together.

PREFACE

Most industrial corporations spend 40 to 70 percent of their pre-tax income on technology. This translates into the allocation of large capital expenditures and human resources towards maintaining, enhancing, and changing the direction of the businesses. Although technology plays such a major role in a corporation's performance, inadequate attention is paid to technological planning and management. Technology as defined here is products, processes, tools and devices, and their organization for use by people in fashioning goods and services. It includes research and development (R&D) but is not limited solely to R&D and encompasses all technical aspects of products and processes along with activities such as technology forecasting, technology licensing, and various support functions which are essential for the development and deployment of technology.

In the current state of planning, the major corporate emphasis is on marketing and financial issues, reflecting short-term financial results, micro-issues, and short-term resource allocation and funding. The position of marketing as a dominant function of business has evolved from the belief that a good marketing department can overcome all the business hurdles. This was the case after World War II, when there was an abundance of demand and fewer competitors. The marketing department was the key to full participation in this boom. Although the role of marketing is still important, the modern environment of vigorous competition, customer sophistication, and quickly advancing technologies emphasizes the need for additional talents in order to remain competitive in the market place. To market a product it must be cost competitive, cost effective, and equal or better in quality and services than the competition can provide.

Today technological attributes, which play an important role in present and future costs and quality of the product, have become dominant criteria in product saleability. Heavy emphasis on marketing alone is not likely to keep a business successful. A combination of both technical and market factors controls the fate of a product line. Since these two functions form the heart of a business, their planning must be done in conjunction with each other, including inputs from both and resulting in an integrated technology/business plan.

Historically, there has been a time lag between the development of technology and its application in the market place. In today's environment, one of the biggest challenges facing corporations is reducing this lag. To do so technologists must understand key concepts of business management and business strategy. By the same token, business management must also understand key concepts of technology management and technology strategy. This will serve to achieve optimum results from technology to enhance the competitive position of businesses.

The essential ingredient for mutual understanding is a cohesive technology plan that is tightly integrated with the business plan. Such a plan addresses both market and technology forces ("Market Pull" and "Technology Push") which impact the competitive position and long term profit potential of a business, as well as factors that are important in the optimum utilization of technology. Some of the main reasons for the development of an integrated plan are to:

- Utilize technology-based resources to create an overall competitive business edge by addressing technology, business, and optimum human resource utilization
- Develop products ahead of the competition in areas of need identified by strategic business planning even though existing techniques fall short of fulfilling that need
- Visualize and respond to future needs and threats beyond the scope of a business plan
- Develop a portfolio of technologies to respond to business threats and opportunities
- Provide a realistic approach to the development of new products and technologies
- Coordinate technology and business philosophies
- Handle environmental, safety and product quality issues before they become a threat.

Today's industrial corporations face a critical challenge from three fronts: maturation/decline of conventional businesses; increased substitution from newly developed products; and heightened competition from developed and newly developing countries, both in domestic and international markets. These issues have become increasingly important in the fast changing environment of global competition. To maintain and enhance their competitive position, corporations have adopted a number of strategic planning techniques, most of which were developed by business consulting companies. The portfolio planning approaches are being used widely by diversified industrial corporations. The portfolio planning provides a mechanism for optimizing existing businesses, but does not address optimum management and utilization of technology and human resources.

This work was undertaken to review key strategic business planning concepts and their impact on business and technology and to bring out factors important in the effective management and utilization of technology and human resources. It does not provide a recipe for a quick fix, but rather, it gives material necessary for a rational process of managing technology in concert with business. Technology cannot be managed effectively unless one understands the strategic business planning process and basis of its development.

The book is divided into three distinct sections. The first section (Chapters 1-3) deals with the origin, concept, and rationale of strategic business planning; the development of various techniques used in evaluating businesses; and the impact of implementing strategic planning on businesses, technology, and human resources. The second section (Chapters 4-6) deals with the management of technology, how it has changed over the decades, its existing status, and future challenges. It also details salient features in the management of technology and the role of top management in the effective utilization of technology. The third section (Chapters 7-10) deals with the role of technology in new business development, either by internal development or acquisition, and the impact of corporate culture on innovation and motivation. It also details the methodology of integrating technology and business planning process and a means of implementing it within a corporation.

The Effective Management of Technology

A Challenge for Corporations

BUSINESS PLANNING — ITS ORIGIN, CONCEPTS, RATIONALE

1234567890

CURRENT STATUS

Eighteen chief executives, heading a range of well regarded U.S. firms, participated in a series of special Conference Board Interviews of 1984.[1] Each one of the CEOs emphasized the need for a more flexible and participative management as a key in developing strategic leadership, which has become essential for the short- and long-term corporate viability. Their key concerns about competition were:

- Technology — communication technology, which is becoming available on a global basis, is impacting all aspects of businesses.
- U.S. corporations are facing fierce global competition.
- Active participation of governments, which are concerned about socio-economic needs of their countries, has changed the nature and boundaries of competition.
- Changing socio-economic and demographic factors have created a strong need for new goods and services, while many conventional markets are declining.

All the CEOs interviewed by the Conference Board expressed their concerns about future uncertainties and a strong need to deploy and redeploy assets to take advantage of opportunities for future growth. In the fast changing environment of products and markets, the involvement of all line executives in the strategic management of businesses is almost a must for continued success.

What is a "Business Strategy"?

All the CEOs who were interviewed at the Conference Board were asked to comment on "business strategy" and "strategic business planning" and how they differed from or related to "long range planning".

One of the CEOs commented as follows:

I've found that the word "strategy" is poorly defined. Some people do use it to mean developing a detailed long range plan that assumes you are going to keep right on doing what you are already doing. But as far as I'm concerned, planning a "strategy" has to do with deciding what you should be doing.

The word really comes to us from the military, where it is used in terms of how to win a battle. It is a matter of out-thinking, out-smarting the enemy — applying your resources where your competition is weakest. In the military, it is often limited to an interaction between you and some known competitor(s).

I think in the business community we have rather lost that narrow sense and now use "strategy" much more broadly as meaning a long-term approach, taking into account environmental changes but with no focus on a limited number of known competitors. The old battle between General Motors and Ford is no longer what we have in mind when we say "strategy." We are using the term much more broadly, but it still does include giving thought to likely moves by all your actual or potential competitors in light of the changing global business environment — a definition of their probable strengths and weaknesses and aligning that profile with our own strengths and weaknesses. Seeing where you have the advantage, and then using it to their general detriment in terms of serving the changing needs of changing markets for the kinds of goods or services you can most effectively and efficiently provide. You don't assume, for example, that only GM and Ford are in the automobile business or that either the production of cars or the market for the cars will be limited by national boundaries. Similarly, you don't assume that any company, including your own, will necessarily stay in exactly the same line of business or pursue their businesses in exactly the same way.

It is global economy now, and you must manage accordingly. What's going on in the whole world will need to be taken into account in deciding on your company's best strategy. This may well include, as it did for us, getting into some different businesses that utilized the company's special strengths. When you do that, of course, you will also need to develop separate strategies for each of the businesses. (pp. 2-4)[1] *Reprinted with permission.*

Business Planning

The role of the corporate planning department in the development and execution of the strategic business planning process has been discussed in the Conference Board report of 1981[2]. This report reviews the changes that have occurred in the corporate planning function from the years 1976 through 1981 and projects expected future changes. During these years, the corporate planning function has not changed *per se*, but its emphasis has been directed towards addressing the future uncertainties in a changing business environment. The important changes in the corporate planning staff have been in their enhanced capability to address the firm's changing needs.

The following comments by three of the participants in the 1981 Conference Board Surveys illustrates the changing role of the planning department:

> Five years ago (in 1976) the emphasis of activities was heavily directed towards establishing reporting and resource allocation procedures. Later, there was greater emphasis on developing appropriate business plans and special studies. More recently, activities for identifying longer range diversification and acquisitions have been more prominent. (pp 7-8)[2] *Reprinted with permission.*

According to this survey, shifts in corporate planning responsibilities are reflected by the following conditions:

- A basic change from operating to strategic mode, although emphasis on the operating part is still equally important. This was accomplished by separating strategic plans from operating budget plans.
- A decentralized planning effort where each strategic business unit is responsible and has the resources needed for the formulation of their strategic plans.
- Fast changing micro and macro factors which include competitive postures and social-economic changes. These have created a strong need for developing, refining, and using forecasting techniques. The results of these forecasts are communicated throughout the organization.
- Marketing research and acquisition becoming a major responsibility of the corporate planning department. This has resulted in its involvement with new ventures and new businesses.

The expected future changes according to the survey are:

- "An increased effort to do what they are doing even better in order to bring true strategic planning to their companies.

- "Deeper involvement with planners in the divisions and business units.
- "Heavier commitment to providing better forecasts and dealing with the significant issues of the future."[2]

The projections made in 1981 have accurately described the changes in corporate planning which occurred over the past five years.

DEVELOPMENT OF STRATEGIC PLANNING CONCEPTS

The use of planning as a technique to improve the effectiveness of a corporation's performance was suggested by Henry Fayol in 1916 who said that "management means looking ahead ... if foresight is not the whole of management, at least it is an essential part of it. To foresee in this context means both to assess the future and make provisions for it."[3] Little attention, however, was paid to the formal process of business planning until the late 1950s.

Planning concepts started gaining popularity in the late 1950s. After the publication *Long Range Planning for Management,*[4] business managers and academics started to pay a great deal of attention to theory and practice of planning in the context of managing corporations and businesses. Planning systems originated within corporations to deal with diverse businesses by predicting the future of each business and providing for the resources required in an orderly fashion. These planning systems were given the name of *long range planning* or *comprehensive planning.*

The second phase in the planning process was *strategic business planning* or *Strategic Planning,* which emphasized directing the corporation's resources into the most promising areas, taking into consideration the present environment and anticipated future.

The third phase in business planning was the development of techniques to explain product/market cost behavior and dynamics of international business competition. These techniques were given the names of *experience curve* and *product life cycle.* The development of these techniques led to what is widely known as portfolio planning concepts, which emphasize the division of a corporation into a portfolio of homogeneous and autonomous businesses. These concepts are widely used by most of the diversified U.S. corporations. The latest phase in the business planning process is *integrative planning* which utilizes the positive contributions of *portfolio planning* but corrects for its deficiencies: not making use of synergistic effects of various businesses, and not addressing internal growth through technology/market integration. Way ahead of these concepts is General Electric, which has enhanced portfolio planning to integrative planning and is shifting from strategic mode to entrepreneurial mode while maintaining the essence of the strategic planning process.

In 1969 George A. Steiner[5] wrote a comprehensive treatise entitled, *Top Management Planning.* This book deals extensively with the planning process from its origin after World War II through the different phases of its development. It addresses all aspects of planning including reasons, rationale, responsibilities, and pitfalls. The illustrations given include comprehensive plans of Kaiser Aluminum and Chemical Corporation, Allstate Insurance, and Magnetic Design Incorporated. It deals with the methodology of the planning process at corporate, business, and different functional levels, including quantitative tools for rational planning, importance of corporate aims, and corporate policy and procedures.

Steiner defined strategic planning as, "the process of determining the major objectives of an organization and the policies and strategies that will govern the acquisition, use and disposition of resources to achieve those objectives"(p. 34).[5] This definition is applicable at all organizational levels within a corporation.

His conceptual model of the overall structure and process of business planning has three components: premises, planning, and implementation and review (p. 33).[5]

Premises

Each corporation satisfies one or more socio-economic needs, either directly or indirectly, by providing goods or services to the market place. These goods and services are the end products of transforming resources and skills to meet social needs. The corporations act as agents for this transformation and are rewarded by society buying their goods and services at prices which include the costs and profits for the corporations. The corporate purpose and objective statements represent the contract with the stockholders. These statements consist of a set of specific quantitative and qualitative criteria against which the accomplishments of the corporation can be evaluated. For example, General Electric's "becoming a world class competitor" is the overall organization purpose, and accomplishing a growth rate of 25 percent higher than GNP is a quantitative financial criterion. These statements tend to be general, act as a rallying point within the corporation, and form a premises of future planning.

It is well recognized that the overall purpose of a corporation is to make money. No business organization can survive any length of time unless it is profitable. The profits are generated by producing and selling goods and services to satisfy socio-economic needs. The values of top management have a profound effect on the employees who are responsible for creating goods and services. If top management has only a financial orientation with no regard for their employees, customers, suppliers, stockholers, and social concerns, such values will adversely impact the viability of the corporation, resulting in the loss of productivity and competitive position. The values of top management also impact areas of future growth for the corporation. Values are interjected into all aspects of planning. For instance, the decision to be the customer's best supplier in an industry depends upon the chief executive's values. These values also impact the means chosen to accomplish this objective.

Planning

The goal of planning is to take advantage of future opportunities and to foresee future threats so that actions can be taken to minimize their impact, while meeting overall corporate objectives. To accomplish these objectives a company must understand and maximize its strengths and overcome its weaknesses.

The formal planning process is essentially a calendar describing various activities and interactions which should take place within different organizational structures. It consists of four stages. The first stage, *objective setting,* defines the strategic direction of the corporation and its subunits including various alternatives. The second stage is *strategic planning* for achieving the objectives. The third stage, *operational plan,* consists of defining short-term objectives of the strategic plan, assigning responsibilities to different organizational units, and resource allocation. The fourth stage is *interaction,* feeding back the functional plans to see if they achieve the objectives. Each of the planning stages relies on strong interaction between corporate, business, and functional levels. Each one of these three management levels has distinct strategic responsibilities.

Implementation and Review

As the various functional elements of the plan are executed it is imperative that the assumptions and logic of the plan be tested against the developing reality. Minor deviations can be revised; major deviations require that the planning process be repeated.

Levels of Strategic Responsibility

Steiner's conceptual model describes the following three levels of strategic responsibility:

Corporate Level

The corporate level of responsibility includes:

1. Business portfolio — selecting the businesses in which the firm will participate including broad expansions, diversifications and acquisition guidelines.
2. Resource allocation — acquiring and allocating resources to strengthen existing business and exploit opportunities for future growth.
3. Set overall objectives for each business including financial criteria and broad marketing criteria
4. Policies for employees, government, and stockholders
5. Organization of the overall management structure of the corporation

Business Level

At the business level, responsibilities involve the areas of:

1. industry assessment
2. competitor assessment
3. business strength analysis
4. product portfolio analysis
5. resource allocation

Functional Level

The functional level of strategic responsibility includes:

1. the determination of the basis on which functions will support the business and corporate strategies; and
2. the integration of different functional plans to assure synergism and optimum support.

RESULTS FROM THE IMPLEMENTATION OF LONG RANGE OR COMPREHENSIVE PLANNING

Expected

The planning process was supposed to accomplish the following: provide long term objectives for the corporation; allow management to simulate the impact of current decisions on future events without committing resources, thus providing a strong tool for making current resource allocations which lead to favorable outcomes; create a strong tool for management and direction of multifaceted corporate activities; provide direction for the future of current businesses; generate a concept of team spirit; identify and exploit opportunities in new business areas; exploit synergism between different businesses; and establish credibility with stockholders.

By 1969, the strategic planning process had gone through a number of changes. As described by Steiner,

> Since the end of World War II, changes in business planning have been as dramatic as any in the entire history of business. They are essentially four in number. First, is the development of comprehensive structured corporate plans. Second, is the widespread creation of planning staffs to help top managers operate formal planning programs. These staffs have been established to help top managers develop comprehensive and well-organized plans on the basis of a specified procedure and produce written plans. The essential characteristics of formal planning are these: plans are prepared on some time cycle on the basis of procedures, are well structured, are comprehensive, are developed by many people in a cooperative effort covering a lengthy time span, and are written. Third, is the development of new and powerful tools and methodological ideas to improve the decision making process inherent in comprehensive planning. Fourth, is the systematic effort to look much further into the future. The total impact on business life of the meshing of these four forces has been and will continue to be enormous. (p.14)[5] *Reprinted with permission.*

During this period, at least 75 percent of the largest industrial companies in the United States had formally organized comprehensive planning programs. As conceptualized by academics, the long-range planning process was too idealistic and theoretical for large diversified companies who found both analytical and administrative problems.

Actual

In the late 1960s, most of the major corporations had grown large, with sales and assets exceeding billions of dollars due to acquisitions and internal development. In addition, most of these corporations had diverse businesses with respect to product/markets and technologies both in the United States and abroad. These businesses were managed through a hierarchy of organizational levels, which consisted of divisions, groups, sectors, and corporate management. A large part of research and development was done at the corporate level, which was organized according to the philosophy of Vannevar Bush, director of scientific research for President Roosevelt: "Scientific progress on a broad front results from the free play of free intellects, working on subjects of their own choice, in the manner indicated by their curiosity for exploration of the unknown."[6]

Division managers' autonomy was limited due to extensive policy manuals and a large dependency on shared resources such as sales, marketing, or manufacturing through group levels. The corporate strategy was essentially the aggregation of various resource commitment decisions to various groups and divisions. These resources included capital and operating budgets, and new product and market development expenses. In most cases, corporate and even sector managers were too far removed to review these decisions other than in financial terms and group vice-president was the highest level manager who could examine the resource allocation in any detail. Even the group vice-president's capability to review, evaluate, and take corrective actions for various operating units was limited by the complexity of interdependencies between various businesses. (p.134)[7]

Business planning was a line responsibility; however, a planning department at the corporate level, had four major functions:

- Assistance to divisions and groups in the preparation of strategic plans including its timely submission, evaluation, and administration
- Economic environmental analysis for the company's businesses
- Combination of divisional plans into a corporate long range plan detailing resource requirements
- Corporate development which consisted of providing assistance to corporate management and the operating units with respect to the evaluation and negotiation of mergers and acquisitions. (p.135)[7]

A five-year forecast, assessing the impact of general economic data and forecasts on products/markets, was prepared by each division. The general economic data was provided by the planning group. The five-year plan consisted of goals and objectives for realizing the market and profit targets which included capital investments, research and development (R&D) expenditure, marketing, manufacturing, and other cost components. In summary, the long-range plans were largely financial projections that contained a five-year income statement and balance sheet. The income statement and, in particular, the next year's income statement received the maximum attention and was the basis of resource allocation. The first year's long range plan became the operating plan for evaluation and control purposes.

In the long-range planning process, corporations influenced various businesses through operational control. There was a minimal amount of strategic influence, and little or no dialogue between divisions and corporate management. The operational units were essentially tactical with a low level of strategic thinking. Such a mode of operation resulted in nondifferentiated management of businesses reflecting resource commitments based on tactical rather than strategic needs.

Strategic and operating control are defined as the processes by which corporate management influences business strategies for long-term profit-potential, and the assurance of realizing that potential respectively. In actual practice, these two processes are interlinked through the same administrative system, and at times are in conflict with each other. Most of the time managers have to make a number of decisions which impact both operational and strategic concerns, and often it is a trade off between the two. Since operational control requires fulfillment of short-term objectives, which forms the basis of a manager's performance evaluation and usually compensation, there is a strong tendency to make decisions based on short-term concerns at the expense of strategic concerns. (p.346)[7]

The overall result of practicing long-range planning within a diversified corporation was skewed imbalance in resource allocation which resulted in the continual subsidization of marginal businesses and underinvestment in growth opportunities.

Continual Subsidization of Marginal Businesses

During the 1950s and 60s, many corporations had diversified in a large number of related and unrelated businesses. This diversification occurred by acquisition and internal development. Factors such as raw material sourcing, competition, growth rate of end use markets, emergence of substitution products, and the cost structure of products/services in various market segments received minimal attention in the long-range planning process. The operating units had the profit and loss responsibility for a number of businesses, which shared common resources. In this structure of management, it was not possible to identify a business in the initial stages of performance problems. Even when the performance problems became obvious, the businesses were either subsidized with the hope of turnaround, or operating management was changed. The initial performance problems of these businesses usually resulted from a lack of management attention to technology, competition, and cost of product/service components to various market segments. By the time these problems were recognized, a large resource allocation, which the corporations were frequently unwilling to commit, was required to turn these businesses around. Organizational and personal commitments often prevented the consideration of divestment as an option. The result was a continued resource drain in an unsuccessful attempt to turn the business around. (p.50)[7]

Underinvestment in Growth Opportunities

The first step toward investment in growth opportunities is to recognize these opportunities based on market share and growth in different market segments. The second step is to commit resources, which include capital investment and strategic expenses. To do so often requires foregoing short term profits and recognizing the risks involved in such businesses. In the process of long range planning, the corporate influence on different businesses was mostly operational, which tended to have a strong focus on short-term profits. The business managers would forgo growth opportunities to meet short-term performance objectives. In addition, businesses were managed with a large number of interdependencies and had trouble focusing on areas of future growth. Successful exploitation of growth business calls for a focused and planned approach with a commitment to deploy resources to meet market needs in a timely fashion. Corporations must assure that management competency exists to use these resources to produce a successful end result. Often corporations have committed large resources to businesses without competent management, resulting in the loss of opportunities.

Growth businesses, by their very nature, tend to have small revenues compared to core businesses, which tend to be mature and have large revenues. This disparity resulted in core business operating managers having a large clout in commanding corporate resources for businesses which had a low return on investment. The overall management structure of the past could be described as decentralized and nondifferentiated, which required uniform performance from all businesses. (p.50)[7]

BUSINESS EVALUATION TECHNIQUES

During the late 1960s corporations consisted of a number of businesses which had little strategic fit. Planning for such businesses was extremely difficult, especially since they were managed as an aggregate of diverse product lines. In many cases it was impossible to account for what resources were assigned to which businesses. Diversified corporations were facing a serious performance problem. Sales were increasing while profits were flat or decreasing. From industry's perspective, specifically, the overall economic/cultural environment was characterized by rapid change in generally unfavorable directions.

- Economic growth rates were declining and duration of recession periods increasing.
- Social values were turning away from economic well being to quality of life issues.
- International competition with West Germany and Japan was becoming intense.
- The growth rate of worker productivity was leveling off.

Many of these factors resulted from the postwar baby boom population reaching adulthood. This group's changing values ushered in the era of government regulation and employee activism. Businesses were now challenged to attract and satisfy stockholders. These challenges created a strong need for the development of techniques to evaluate different businesses or product lines for their growth and profit potential as a basis for resource allocation. Most of the resultant techniques were developed by business consulting firms and originated from the concepts of experience curve and product life cycle.

Experience Curve

The term *experience curve* is attributed to the Boston Consulting Group (BCG)[8]. The initial work by BCG was done in 1965 and 1966 and was first used to explain the price and competitive behavior of the fast growing market segments of the chemical and electronics industry. They observed that the cost of a product goes down as the company's experience in production and marketing increases. The name chosen by BCG was selected to distinguish it from the learning curve effect, which was discovered in 1925 at Wright Patterson Airforce Field. The learning curve relates to the direct labor costs required to perform a task, which decreases as people performing the task become familiar with it, thus increasing their efficiency. The experience curve on the other hand includes other costs in addition to the labor cost. According to Jain

> Cost characteristics of the experience curve can be observed in all types of costs, whether they are labor costs, advertising costs, overhead costs, marketing costs, development costs, or manufacturing costs. Also the cost derivatives of the curve are not based on accounting costs, but on the accumulated cash input divided by the accumulated end product output. The cost decline of the experience curve is the rate of change in that ratio.[9]

The experience curve can be expressed mathematically by the Cobb-Douglas function:

$$Cn = C_1 n^{-\lambda}$$

where:

Cn = Cost of nth unit
C_1 = Cost of first unit
n = Accumulated volume
λ = a constant, based on the degree of experience

This equation when plotted on a log-log curve is a straight line, if the effects of inflation have been removed and costs and prices are stated in real terms. Three main factors are responsible for the existence of the experience curve: learning, technology, and economy of scale. The learning factor explains the phenomenon that as experience is gained in the field of production, marketing, and sales, the efficiency increases and is reflected in a lower cost of the product. Improvements in technology yield reductions of both fixed and variable costs and overall result in lower manufacturing costs. The economy of scale effects apply to a majority of manufacturing processes. An increase in capacity seldom requires an equivalent increase in other costs such as capital, operating, or overhead. For instance the chemical and allied industry follows a 0.6 rule expressed by the following equation:

$$C_2 = \text{The capital cost for capacity } S_2 = C_1(S_2/S_1)^{0.6}$$
$$\text{where } S_2 < S_1 \text{ or } S_2 > S_1$$

and C_1 is the capital cost for capacity S_1.

BCG observed that the cost decreases by 22 to 30 percent for every doubling of experience as measured by cumulative production volume.

A hypothetical example of the experience curve is shown in Figure 1.1, where the vertical axis is the log of cost or price and the horizontal axis is the cumulative number of units produced.

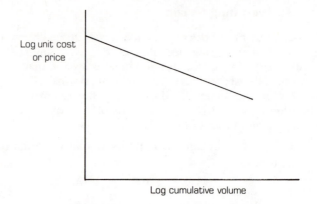

Log unit cost or price

Log cumulative volume

Figure 1.1   The Experience Curve

Two key questions must be addressed when evaluating the experience curve.

    1.   What does it mean?
    2.   What is its reliability?

The cost/volume or price/volume slopes indicate relative learning power over time, and can be quantitatively related to each other. Theoretically, if complete cost information is available, ie, fixed, variable, and cost of sales, along with market share, it can provide an insight to the competitive cost of a product and can be compared with one's own product line. The information can be used to guide present and future pricing of the product to gain strategic advantage. However, the information required to generate experience curves of competition is almost impossible to obtain, and in many cases even one's own cost structure is hard to assess except on a long-term basis.

The strategic importance of the experience curve lies in its relationship to the growth of a product. If a product is not growing, the production stays constant, and the rate of cost decline per year gradually slows down and approaches zero. If such is the case, even an increase in market share due to the disappearance of a competitor will have only temporary and limited benefits in mature, no growth products which ultimately face a declining market. (p.32)[8]

The experience curve further emphasizes the importance of market share in the growth industry, where a gain in market share is the key to success. The increased market share, according to the experience curve, results in decreasing costs and provides high profit margins. This phenomenon was observed somewhat in the high growth business of the late 1960s, but it has become epitomized by the semiconductor businesses of the 1980s. A company which is six months late in introducing a chip of new design cannot produce the product for the price the first entrant is now selling at.

In summary BCGs experience curve is a hypothesis derived from an observed phenomenon in a large number of product lines, which indicated that every doubling in experience reduced the cost of a product by 22 to 30 percent. In the strategic management of product lines, such an observation had strong implications on the importance of growth rate and market share. It implies that mature products will have a low return on investment, whereas products with high growth rates, despite a negative or low initial return on investment, will generate high profits as a result of increasing market share and a decrease in costs due to gained experience.

Day and Montgomery reviewed implications in development of the experience curve and some of the delusions that arose by using it as a strategic tool.[10,11] They detail the implications of the experience curve concepts to competitive analysis as well as some of the discontinuities which can occur.

Two such discontinuities which can occur in the experience curve are deployment of capital for noneconomic programs such as environmental and safety, and major cost reduction or capacity expansions. In the case of an unsuccessful program, the costs can actually go up depending upon the magnitude of cash deployed and penalties in the operating cost. The impact of these factors on costs is shown in Figure 1.2.

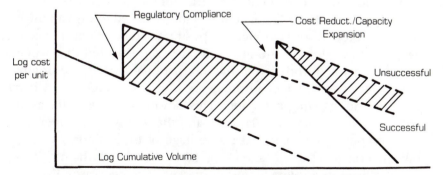

Figure 1.2   Discontinuities in the Experience Curve

According to the experience curve, a leader in the market place should have an advantage over followers; however, numerous instances occur where this is not true. Such has been the case in copying machines, automobiles, cameras, and other industries where the Japanese were followers yet took away a major market share from the leaders. This can occur when:

- the follower takes advantage of the mistakes made by the leader, both in the market place and process technology.
- dissemination of a product leads to the design and development of a better or cheaper product. The Japanese have done this successfully.
- developing improved technology with cheaper raw materials or a better efficiency leads to a considerable cost advantage — technological leap-frog.

In fact with fast developing technologies, a leader has to make a concentrated effort to maintain his advantage and any sloppiness in resource utilization will have strong adverse impacts.

Product Life Cycle

First discussed in comprehensive detail by Raymond Vernon[12] during the 1960s, the product life cycle model was influenced by the ideas of a number of individuals, particularly Irving Kravis,[13] who had published earlier works involving the concept. The model was tested and refined by a others, including Louis Wells, Robert Stobaugh, and John E. Tilton.[14] According to the product life cycle model, a product goes through different stages of development: conception; market acceptance; growth; and maturity, where supply and demand are balanced; and decline, the final state that occurs as new, more cost effective products are developed, gain consumer acceptance, and displace the original product. The extent of decline depends upon market segments penetrated by new products.

The product life cycle concept was initially used to explain the behavior of international competitive position of different products, vis-a-vis their position on the life cycle. It was postulated that when a new product is introduced in the international market, the originating country has a distinct advantage resulting from technology barriers, such as patent protection. This advantage disappears as the technologies become standardized and the world market increases. The competing countries take advantage of the economy of scale, raw material positioning, and cheap labor. As a result, the innovating country loses its advantage, and its market share decreases. Eventually, the country where the product originated may even lose its domestic market to imports from other countries.[15] The U.S. television industry is illustrative of this hypothesis, first losing market share to the Japanese companies, which in turn are losing market share to Korean and Taiwanese manufacturers.

New products originate primarily in developed countries, having superior technological capabilities. In the past the United States has been a prime innovator of new products and has successfully exploited this strength by using large domestic markets to reduce the cost of innovation, since only a small percentage of the ultimate market is necessary for success.[16] In recent years, however, Japan has more successfully penetrated the U. S. market (by introducing new and innovative products based on the U. S. market needs) than U. S. corporations. Japan's advantage has been based on quality, price, and correct assessment of market needs.

The industrialized countries consider product life cycle to be a dynamic process in which markets are lost in some areas and new ones are generated in others. The developed countries maintain and enhance the market lead either by process or product innovations using their strong technological base.[17] In recent years, fast technological developments have decreased the life cycle of new products, and advantages from innovations are more likely to be short term than long term. Hence, a strong effort in developing and deploying technology in the market is a must for continuing success in a global competitive environment.

Strategic Implications

The concepts of experience curve and product life cycle resulted in some conclusions regarding new products in the market. When a new product is introduced, its cost goes down with the gain in experience, which is a function of growth rate. Different pricing strategies can be implemented, depending upon the nature of the product, its growth rate, and intensity of competition. Based on the knowledge of the experience curve, the initial market price could be set at a price lower than cost, but as the market grows with product acceptance, this trend is reversed. The cost goes down faster than price, providing large profit margins to the industry leader. This strategy will attract more competitors. The new competitors may have smaller margins, but the business will be profitable for all. When cost and price are not adjusted, the overall result is an unstable condition, with too many competitors compared to the size of the total market. This situation is further destabilized due to the introduction of more cost effective substitution products. The overall result is a shakeout in the industry.

Such has been the case in the soda ash industry. In the 1970s, the five manufacturers of natural soda ash — FMC Corporation, Allied Corporation, Stauffer Chemical Company, Texas Gulf Industries in Wyoming; and Kerr McGee Corporation in California, were all enjoying relatively high profit margins. In addition Allied had a synthetic soda ash plant in Syracuse, New York. All were at the verge of expansions based on general speculation that European synthetic soda ash plants would be closed due to their dependence on high cost energy. The manufacturing technology for natural soda ash had become standard and readily available, so that the only barrier to entry was high capital. In the late 70s, Tenneco, with a lot of cash from their oil businesses, built a one million ton per year plant. During the same period, plastic bottles were being introduced as a substitute for glass, the single largest market for soda ash, and European plants were modernized and supported by the common market. The result: a declining soda ash market, a price war, and the closing of the Allied Syracuse plant. Even today, a once highly profitable business finds itself struggling to break even.

Steven C. Wheelwright[18] provides additional examples of the use of experience curve and product life cycle as practiced by Texas Instruments (TI) and Hewlett-Packard (HP). According to Wheelwright, "TI favors early entry, followed by expansion and consolidation of its position, resulting in a dominant market share when the product matures. HP, on the other hand, tends to create new markets, but then exits (or introduces other new products) as cost driven competitors enter and the market matures. TI empasizes continual price cuts to parallel cost reductions in order to build volume and take advantage of experience curve. HP, on the other hand, puts less emphasis on manufacturing cost reductions and holds prices longer so that profit margins expand during the initial periods. The early returns generated allow early exit from the market with good returns on investment and provide funds for further product and research development."

SUMMARY

Planning concepts started gaining popularity in the 1950s. After the publication of *Long Range Planning for Management,* business managers and academics started to pay a great deal of attention to the theory and practice of planning in context with managing corporations and businesses. The initial planning concepts were termed *long range planning* or *comprehensive planning.* These concepts assumed that corporations would continue to be doing what they were doing in their products and services. The underlying reason for this assumption was a stable market based on the pent up demand of World War II and driven by the postwar growth and economic well being. Competition was almost exclusively domestic.

By the mid 1960s, the recovery of Western Europe and Japan from the impact of World War II was well under way. As a result of this recovery, U.S. corporations started feeling the impact of foreign competition both in national and international markets. The competitive pressures created a strong need for the development of new techniques for understanding market dynamics. The concepts of *product life cycle* and *experience curve* were developed to meet this need and were originally used to explain international market dynamics and cost/price behavior of different product lines. In the late 1960s, these concepts gained widespread recognition in the majority of U.S. corporations as a means of strategy formulation. Their usefulness, however, was limited for diversified corporations, which consisted of a large number of related and unrelated businesses and had a strong need for the identification of profit potential and resource allocation.

REFERENCES

1. Shaeffer, R.G.: *Developing strategic leadership.* Conference Board Report No. 847, 1984, pp. 1-15.

2. O'Connor R.: The corporate planning department responsibility and staffing.Conference Board Report No. 806, 1981, pp. 1-8.

3. Fayol, H.: *General and Industrial Management.* Pitman Publishing Corp., New York, 1949, p. 43.

4. Ewing, D.W. (ed.): *Long Range Planning for Management.* rev. ed. Harper & Row, New York, 1964.

5. Steiner, G.A.: *Top Management Planning.* Macmillan, New York, 1969.

6. Bush, V.: Science — The Endless Frontier. July 1945; Reprint edition by Arno Press Inc. 1980.

7. Haspeslagh, P.C.: Portfolio Planning Approaches and the Strategic Management Process in Diversified Industrial Companies. Ph.D. Thesis, Harvard Business School, 1983.

8. *Perspectives on Experience Curve,* The Boston Consulting Group Inc, 1968.

9. Jain, S.C.: *Marketing, Planning and Strategy.* South-Western, Cincinnati, Ohio, 1981. p. 209.

10. Day, G.S., Montgomery, D.B.: Diagnosing The Experience Curve, *Journal of Marketing* 47: 44-58, 1984.

11. Kiechel, W.: The Decline of Experience Curve. *Fortune,* October 1981, pp. 139-146.

12. Vernon, R.: International Investment and International Trade in the Product Life Cycle. *Quarterly Journal of Economics* 80,: 190-207, 1966.

13. Kravis, I.: Availability and Other Influence on the Commodity Composition of Trade. *Review of Economics and Statistics* 38: 14-30, 1956.

14. Tilton, J.E.: *International Diffusion of Technology, The Case of Semiconductors,* The Brookings Institution, Washington D.C., 1971.

15. Lutz, J.M., Green, R. T.: The Product Life Cycle and the Export Position of the United States. *Journal of International Business Studies,* Winter 1983, pp. 77-93.

16. Sebastian, M.A.: The Product Life Cycle Theory: Empirical Evidence. *Journal of International Business Studies,* Winter 1983, pp. 95-102.

17. Walker, W.B.: *Industrial Innovation and International Trading Performance: Contemporary Studies in Economic and Financial Analysis.* Jai Press, Greenwich, CT, 1979, p. 15.

18. Wheelwright, Steven C.: Strategy, Management, and Strategic Planning Approaches. *Interfaces* 14: 24-25, 1984.

DEVELOPMENT OF PORTFOLIO PLANNING CONCEPTS

1 2 3 4 5 6 7 8 9 10

HISTORICAL PERSPECTIVE OF BUSINESS PLANNING

After World War II, the United States enjoyed a predominant position in the world markets, resulting in a euphoria as reflected by this excerpt from George Steiner.

> After World War II, a powerful new idea became generally accepted that businesses no longer stood helpless in the face of market forces. A company could, according to this new idea, in the words of Ernest Breech at the time he was Chairman of the Board of Ford Motor Company, "make trends . . . not follow them." He went on to say that "With a well-staffed management team in which an aggressive risk-taking spirit is backed up by cool-headed analytical planning there will be no problem too tough to be solved." (Breech in Barsk and Fenn, Jr., 1956, p. 17*)This is a philosophy that businesses can, to a great degree, determine where they want to go in the future and do things that assure their objectives are achieved. (pp. 15-16)[1] *Reprinted with permission.*

U.S. corporations had a free access to a number of technologies which were developed during World War II. When commercialized, these technologies provided the corporations with strong competitive advantages over Europe and Japan, which were recovering from the effects of World War II.

As the economic recovery proceeded throughout the world, most of the technologies were standardized. In many cases, as Japan and Western Europe began building their manufacturing facilities, they

*From *Planning the Future Strategy of Your Business* by Edward C. Brust and Dan. H. Fenn, Jr., Copyright 1956 by McGraw-Hill Book Company, Inc.

improved over the standard technologies practiced in the United States. As a result, the United States began to lose its share in international markets, and in some instances, even in domestic markets to Europe and Japan.

The competitiveness of U.S. manufacturing was further hampered in the 1970s, when government imposed a number of strict legislations to improve the environment and enhance worker safety. Large amounts of both financial and human resources had to be deployed to meet these noneconomic regulatory pressures, resulting in an increased cost of goods.

For these reasons, things have changed considerably over the last two decades in the arena of international competition. Japan and West Germany have developed and successfully deployed strong technological capabilities in a wide variety of areas to enhance standardized technologies for cost reduction and product improvement. Further, they have been successful in penetrating international markets, including the United States, by recognizing and exploiting market niches which U.S. corporations have ignored. An example of this change can be found in the marketing of copying machines for small customers and accounting firms, which Xerox refused to recognize and serve as being too small and specialized. Timex, a one time leader in watches, provides another example, having lost market dominance to the Japanese. Kodak has met the same fate in the camera market. In manufacturing industries, steel is a glaring example, where a one time world leader like U.S. Steel has problems staying competitive. Overall, the attitude of the U.S. corporation toward consumers had been insensitive, providing an opportunity for competition to step in and better serve this huge market. In addition, Japan has done a superior job in integrating technology and business functions, providing them with a strong advantage by being more cost effective and reducing the time lag between developing and marketing new products.

At present, corporations are faced with two major sources of competition: 1) technologically advanced Japan and West Germany, which are becoming leaders in the introduction of new and improved products; and 2) new developing countries with cheap labor and easy access to standardized technology who are dominating conventional markets.

These factors resulted in a change in the dynamics of the market place, which impacted the stability of U.S. corporations. The outcome has been an internal struggle for mergers, leveraged buy outs, and the emergence of corporate raiders. Such actions, when looked upon as to the overall strength of the nation, tend to have a destructive impact on the United States due to their adverse effect on employee morale and productivity, which is easy to destroy but extremely hard to rebuild.

Since 1970, then, the changing worldwide market and domestic environment has dramatically affected corporations and the way they do business. One major way businesses have been trying to face these challenges is by the introduction and use of a variety of strategic business planning techniques. *Portfolio planning* is a technique that has gained widespread acceptance and is being used by a majority of diversified corporations.

PORTFOLIO PLANNING

Philippe C. Haspeslagh, as a part of his Ph.D. thesis at the Harvard Business School conducted extensive research on portfolio planning and its implementation within diversified industrial corporations. According to Haspeslagh's research up to 1979, an estimated 53 percent among the diversified companies in the Fortune 500 ranking and 42 percent among the diversified companies in the Fortune 1000 ranking had adopted these portfolio planning approaches.[2] Today the number of companies using these techniques is much higher.[3]

Haspeslagh examined the use of portfolio planning by corporations in influencing business strategies. Portfolio planning provided top corporate management with a means to address two major issues of diversified companies: "how to allocate resources across many widely different businesses when it is impossible to be familiar with all the relevant aspects of their strategic position, and how to influence multiple business unit strategies and coordinate them into an overall corporate strategy to maximize long-term profitability?" (p.4)[2]

It must be emphasized, however, that two areas of major importance within a corporation are not addressed in the portfolio concept: 1) the management of interdependencies across various businesses, important in exploiting synergistic effects of markets and technologies; and 2) future growth by internal development, an important part in the management of technology. Thus, portfolio planning must be only a *part* of corporate strategy, since it does not address two major areas that are vital to the long-term viability of the corporation.

Other important conclusions of Haspeslagh's work can be summarized as follows:

- For practical purpose all portfolio models are the same and their application involves considerable judgement.
- The portfolio planning is triggered by performance crisis.
- Portfolio planning approaches are most widely used by diversified industrial corporations which manage multiple interdependencies and have high asset businesses.
- The practical application of portfolio concepts differs significantly from theory. Theoretically, each strategic business unit (SBU) is defined as homogeneous and autonomous, and is assigned a position in the portfolio matrix with a strategic mission for which resources are directly allocated. In practice, however, the SBUs are neither completely autonomous nor homogeneous. Rather, they are organizational units consisting of a portfolio of strategic segments, each segment having a mission, and resources are allocated to these segmented missions.
- Portfolio planning systems differ from previous long-range planning systems in four ways. They provide a stronger strategic control influence over business units; they provide direct dialogue between businesses and corporate level; they require strategic thinking at business level; and they emphasize differentiation in strategic control influence across businesses.
- The introduction of portfolio planning calls for a differentiation in strategic and operational control.
- The implementation of portfolio planning requires a way of thinking radically different than past practices, resulting in a long educational process which could take three to five years.
- The implementation of portfolio concepts has a strong impact on resource allocation. Improvement in financial performance cannot be directly related to portfolio planning, particularly when performance problems triggered the use of portfolio concepts.
- The introduction of the portfolio planning process increases corporate influence over businesses but does not address interdependence and growth strategy.

All in all, Haspeslagh's work illustrated that the portfolio strategy is only one component of a diversified corporation's strategy. The other major components which are interdependence strategy and renewal or growth strategy must be integrated with portfolio strategy through the process of corporate influence. (pp.14–15)[2]

The most influential academic contribution to portfolio planning is Michael Porter's work on structural analysis of industry and competitive position.[4] According to this analysis, profitability of an industry is determined by the intensity of competition. Not a random phenomenon, competition arises out of industry structure which is controlled by five elements:

1. threat of new entry which limits profit margins
2. threat of substitution which limits prices
3. the relative bargaining power of suppliers
4. the relative bargaining power of buyers
5. the intensity of rivalry between competition. (pp.65–66)[2]

Porter's work also deals with what he calls *generic strategy* which relates return on investment, market share, and characteristics of the market. Market is segmented into three distinct strategic areas.

- Overall Cost Leadership — In this strategy, high return on investment is generated by selling standard products at low cost with low profit margin, but to a large market. The overall result is a high return on investment.
- Differentiated Product — This strategy recommends specialized products, which are sold on perceived quality and performance differences. The market segment may be small but is willing to pay a high price for such products. The net result is a high return on investment.
- Focus — In this strategy, there is concentration on certain niches, either a particular group of customers, a geographic area, distribution or any other specialized niche.

In the Conference Board report No. 876 on Competitive Leverage, Furrer[5] describes strategy formulation as attaining the ultimate objective of business success as measured by superior return on investment and cash flow. He classified businesses in three distinct categories based on customer needs. For businesses that serve customers with numerous needs, the competitive advantage lies in identifying those needs and providing a unique product or service to satisfy them. Price is not the key issue; it is the uniqueness of the product that gives superior performance. An example of these types of businesses are ethical drugs. In the second category of businesses, customer needs are well defined and known to all competing participants. In this case price is the key criterion for successful performance. Many commodity businesses fall into this category. Here the focus is on controlling costs. Profitability is obtained by product differentiation and economy of scale. In many businesses, however, neither product differentiation nor economies of scale provides an advantage. These businesses, which comprise the third group, have no strategic thrust, but the emphasis is on operating skill which is an outcome of management competency.

Furrer also classifies business on a 3x3 competition/customer matrix. According to his estimate, 10 to 20 percent of the firms have good to superior return on investment; 40 to 60 percent of firms have poor to fair returns; and 30 to 40 percent have poor returns with fair to good returns occasionally possible.

The market function is to identify, evaluate, and recommend the strategy. Technology provides a cost effective means of supporting that strategy by cost reduction, product differentiation and development of unique products to satisfy customer needs. For a successful strategic development and deployment, early involvement of marketing and technology is a must. In addition, both technology and marketing must have the right mix of skills and talents based upon the particular strategic thrust. This is more important in technology, since the skills and talents which can support one strategy, such as cost reduction, are not capable of providing strong support to product differentiation or development of new and unique products.

If the strategic thrust of a product line or business is determined as a continued and long-term superior return on investment and cash flow, an integrated technology/business thrust is a basic requirement. How to provide this thrust in a cost effective mode, particularly in a diversified corporation, is the biggest challenge for top management. The portfolio concepts do not address the management of technologies. General Electric recognized the limitation of portfolio concepts by 1974 and moved towards a more integrated structure by creating sectors which contained a number of SBUs. GE further recognized that emphasis on business issues alone does not address strategic concerns in its entirety, particularly those relating to technology.

To change from business specific issues to common themes, GE introduced the concept of *corporate planning challenge*. Each year one specific issue was tackled, starting with the strengthening of technological capability. Reginald Jones, CEO of General Electric at the time, remarked:

> For example as a defrocked bookkeeper, I have always had a concern about technology. I commissioned a company wide study of our strengths, weaknesses, and needs in technology. The findings — sixteen volumes of them — triggered a technological renaissance in GE.

We stepped up our recruiting and training activities. Now every SBU has a firm technological strategy integrated within its business strategy.[6] *Reprinted with permission.*

No general solution for managing technology in a diversified corporation can be given since the management of technology is highly dependent upon the nature of the businesses. But, it must be recognized that portfolio planning concepts do not address the optimum management of technology. Each corporation must address the technology issue separately to assure that it is being managed to provide the proper tactical and strategic thrust to all the businesses.

Definition of Portfolio Planning

Portfolio planning approaches are based on the recognition that a diversified company consists of a number of businesses. Each one of these businesses is required to stand on its own merit and contribute towards overall corporate objectives and should be managed accordingly.

The practical application of portfolio planning consists of the following four steps:

- Reexamination of various businesses within a corporation for strategic formulation by considering products/markets. The resulting units may or may not coincide with the existing operating units and are given the name of Strategic Business Units (SBUs).
- Classifying the businesses in a "portfolio matrix" according to industry attractiveness and business strength.
- Assigning each SBU a strategic mission depending upon its growth and profit potential.
- Allocating resources to each business based on the above evaluations. (p. 62)[2]

Portfolio planning models deemphasize interdependencies among various businesses, with the exception of cash flow which is pooled across businesses. The portfolio concept advocates balancing the cash flow among the portfolio of businesses, mature businesses providing cash for growth businesses, which as they mature would become a source of cash to new growth businesses. The portfolio concepts rely on the fact that cash generation and management within a corporation, where management expertise in deploying and controlling cash is better, is more efficient than obtaining cash from external capital markets. In addition, the growth businesses may not be able to raise capital from external markets when needed, and mature businesses having excess cash may not be able to invest it for maximum return. The portfolio planning models provide a methodology for evaluating different businesses' growth and profit potential based on industry attractiveness and business strength, and help top management balance the cash flow between businesses.

Definition of Strategic Business Unit (SBU)

The traditional long range planning took organizational operating units for granted, whereas the portfolio planning concept emphasizes a need for reexamination of businesses' structure for strategic planning purposes. In 1971 General Electric introduced the concept of strategic business units after reexamining its operating units and discovering a high degree of interdependencies, which made it extremely difficult to assess the resource allocation and profit potential of individual businesses.[7] The company, therefore reorganized its 9 groups, 48 divisions and 150 departments into 43 SBUs, many of which crossed traditional group, divisional and operating lines. The SBUs were formulated on two basic principles. First, the businesses must be defined as the smallest possible unit which is independent for strategic planning purposes. Second, resources should be allocated directly to the units to support these businesses. These SBUs became the focus of formal planning and resource allocation. For example, three separate divisions of household appliances were merged into a single SBU serving the "household market." (p.70)[2]

The definition of SBU is critical to portfolio planning. The traditional market segmentation consisted of serving a group of customers with similar needs, then tailoring the product to satisfy that niche. This focused business effort on differentiation for competitive advantage. One type of differentiation is to fill a gap in the market not served by the industry leader; another type of segmentation strategy is to compete against the industry leader by price skimming and/or product improvement. Such forms of segmentation are tactical and based on customer needs, and ignore the cost considerations. As a result, this type of segmentation does not erect economic barriers against the eventual entry of lower cost producers. In portfolio planning the segmentation is based on cost considerations in serving customers and results in a competitive advantage. (p.70)[2] To accomplish this product/markets are analyzed for the following characteristics:

1.   Regrouping of customer needs and analyzing them for eco-

nomic value from customer's point of view

2. Analyzing the business's cost structure relative to the competition in serving those needs

3. Exploiting some other advantage — differentiated product or strong patent position. (p.71)[2]

Such analysis leads to the recognition of each market segment for product/service need. Since each component of the service adds to the delivered cost of the product, by tailoring product/service components according to market segmentation, the products can be supplied at a lower cost than an unfocused approach.

Based on these concepts, Haspeslagh[8] defines SBUs in three common ways. The first approach consists of five steps.

- Examine the product's economic value to different market segments and compare it with the full delivered cost to that segment.

- Complete the value added analysis to examine the total delivered cost structure of servicing these various segments and the extent to which the cost elements are distinct or shared with other activities.

- Assess the cost/volume relationship for the various components of the cost structure; this is often accomplished through experience curve analysis.

- Compare the relative cost position of the various competitors.

- Optimize product/service components for each market segment to provide a cost advantage over competition. (pp.72–73)[2]

These steps lead to delineating or aggregating various market segments into a single SBU.

"The second way of defining an SBU ... is to examine the market to determine if it contains successful competitors who are in that given business only. If such competitors do exist, the business is considered to be an SBU.

"The third way ... is to examine to what extent a unit can afford to control its own critical resources such as sales organization, production facilities, engineering, etc." (p.73)[2]

The ideal SBU, according to the portfolio management concept, should be completely independent in the areas of: profit and cash flow, manufacturing/technology, marketing, customer service, human resource utilization and development, and strategic planning. In addition it should have a minimum need for interaction with other decentralized profit centers.

Portfolio Classification of SBUs

"Once the SBUs have been defined, the second step in all portfolio planning models is the classification of these SBUs using some form of matrix." (p.74)[2] The matrices are characterized by industry attractiveness and business strength of the product/market. The purpose of this display is to evaluate the relative position of different businesses in the overall corporate portfolio. The four best known portfolio planning strategic models are Boston Consulting Group's growth/share matrix, Strategic Planning Institute's profit improvement market strategy, Arthur D. Little's business profile matrix and GE/McKinsey's industry attractiveness/business strength matrix.

Boston Consulting Group's (BCG) Growth-Share Matrix

Based on their experience curve studies, BCG designed a four-box matrix as a portfolio model[9] (Fig. 2.1). The vertical axis represented market growth and the horizontal axis market share of a product line. The market share is defined as ratio of a company's share in a product line divided by the share of strongest competitor in the industry. BCG uses a somewhat arbitrary dividing line for a relative market share of 1 and a real growth rate of 10 percent which results in a two-by-two matrix. Market growth essentially portrays cash use, and market share signifies cash generation. The BCG matrix is based on the philosophy that cash flow follows the same cycle as a product life cycle. As long as the growth rate of a product exceeds the return on investment, the business will have a negative cash flow. Eventually when the product reaches maturity, the need for added capital diminishes and if the business is profitable, the cash flow is positive.

Each SBU is analyzed for its growth rate and relative market share. Depending upon the values of the these factors, the business unit is assigned a position in the matrix. Each of the boxes has certain characteristics and a recommended strategy for management. Businesses are classified in four categories based on the market share and growth potential and are labelled as *stars, problem child or question mark, dogs,* and *cash cows.*

Star These businesses are characterized by dominant market share with high growth. They are recommended for the greatest resource

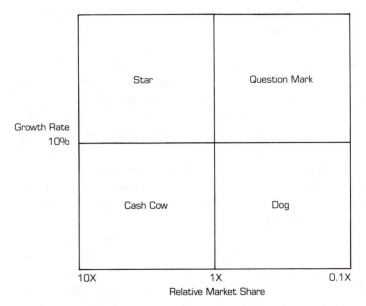

Figure 2.1   BCG's Growth/Share Matrix[9]

allocation because they have the highest growth potential and require more capital for building extra capacity, supporting a higher technology budget, and providing more resources for marketing and sales. Efficiency or effectiveness is a minor criteria; in fact, the strategy propagates the concept of gaining market share at the expense of efficiency or effectiveness. Although the net cash flow in such businesses is usually negative, if a dominant share can be maintained until growth slows, the product will become a high dollar earner. An attempt to extract high earnings during the growth phase will usually result in the loss of dominant position and could ultimately move the product into the *dog* category.

Problem Child A business with high growth rate and low market share is defined as a *problem child,* and the recommended strategy is to infuse more cash to gain share. Such businesses have a negative cash flow. This type of business must achieve a dominant position before growth slows down or it will become marginal. Such businesses demand heavy commitment of both financial and managerial resources, which limits their number in the portfolio.

Dog These businesses have a low market share, low growth rate, a slightly positive to negative cash flow, and demand excessive management attention. The recommended strategy for these businesses is divestiture or liquidation.

Cash Cow Businesses with dominant market share but low growth rate, also termed as mature businesses, fall in this category. These are core businesses of major corporations and tend to have a large positive cash flow. Although not attractive for significant investment, this type of business is the main source of earnings and cash to support growth areas.

The theory behind the matrix is that the excess cash of *cash cows* should be used to fund selected *question marks* or on research and development to create *stars* which as their market matures, will generate more cash and continue the funding cycle.

The overall result of using the BCG matrix is to identify the nature of each business based on growth/market share and assign resources accordingly. In the late 1960s and early 1970s, organizations were staffed to evaluate each business and determine its position in the BCG matrix, which determined the strategy of managing that business.

Profit Improvement Market Strategy (PIMS) by Strategic Planning Institute (SPI)

PIMS is an ongoing statistical study of strategic and performance variables for strategic business units (SBUs). It is based on multiple regression analysis of data on more than fourteen hundred businesses provided by over two hundred participating corporations. The studies are carried out on business results of three to five years.[10,11] A set of general rules are developed to help managers identify critical issues in their businesses. Thirty-seven factors have been isolated which explain about 80 percent of the variation in return on investment of these businesses. Some of the important variables include: investment intensity, market share/growth, quality, productivity, innovation and/or differentiation, vertical integration, and cost escalation. The usefulness of these variables in developing a marketing strategy is illustrated by considering two variables vs. profitability. (p.14)[12]

Capital Intensity vs. Profitability PIMS evaluation of a wide variety of businesses indicates an inverse relationship between the capital intensity of a business and its profitability; that is, the higher the capital intensity, the poorer the return on investment.

Low capital intensity businesses respond well to the following strategies:

1. Being a leader in the strategically important market segments and not diluting effort by participating in all market
segments
2. Placing strong effort on market support and product differentiation
3. Emphasizing product quality
4. Maintaining a high market share in the total market.
(p.14)[12]

On the other hand, these strategies are relatively ineffective in low
capital intensity businesses:

1. Investing capital for vertical integration
2. Assigning resources on aggressive cost reduction, at the expense of marketing and product differentiation. (p.14)[12]

Market Share vs. Profitability The PIMS studies confirmed BCG
findings on market share and profitability. The general recommended
strategies in businesses with relatively high market share include:

1. Placing strong effort on marketing program
2. Maintaining high product quality
3. Developing differentiated products and continuing an effort
to maintain high market share in strategically important
market segments. (p.15)[12]

Basically, SPI's results confirmed BCG's findings and evaluated the
impact of additional variables on the profitability of various businesses.

Arthur D. Little — Industry
Life Cycle Strategic Analysis

Arthur D. Little developed an industry life cycle planning system
by dividing industries into four distinct segments: *embryonic,
growth, mature,* and *aging.*[13] Each segment is characterized by distinct marketing and business strategies. The life cycle stage of an industry depends upon the level and rate of change of the following factors: growth rate/potential, product line breadth/activity,
competitors number/structure, customers loyalty, market share
distribution/stability, ease of entry, and technology focus/stability.

Some industries at different stages of the life cycle are shown in
Figure 2.2.

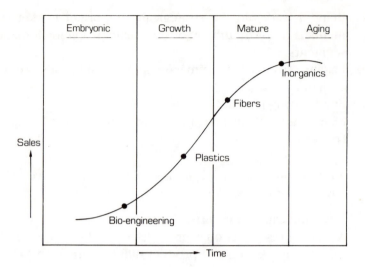

Figure 2.2　Industry Maturity Stages[13]

Reprinted with permission.

According to the life cycle planning concepts, the deployment of cash is a function of a product or business's position on the life cycle. Figure 2.3 depicts the management of cash flow by harvesting businesses in the late mature or aging stage and reinvesting it in research and development (R&D), marketing, and manufacturing facilities for embryonic and growth businesses. This essentially provides a balanced cash flow and a means of continued new business development.

BCGs growth share-matrix and PIMS do not address the effect of competition at different life cycle stages of a product. Arthur D. Little's Industry-Maturity-Competitive matrix was designed to evaluate and recommend business characteristics of a product at different stages of its life cycle vis-a-vis competition and to recommend strategies. The businesses are classified on a 5x4 matrix as shown in Figure 2.4.[13] The vertical axis is a plot of competitive position and the horizontal axis is industry's life cycle to which the product belongs. The position in the twenty column matrix indicates what strategy should be followed. In this analysis, competitive position is determined by a combination of three factors: market share, competitive economics, and factors which usually reflect the present strength and weakness of the business.

The Industry-Maturity-Competitive position matrix characterizes competitive position by five classifications.

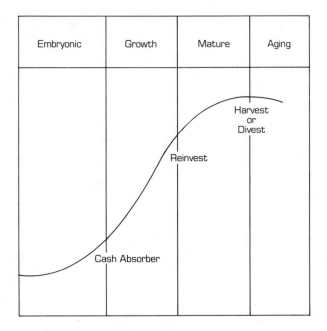

Figure 2.3   Cash Deployment Over Life Cycle[13]

Reprinted with permission.

- *"Dominant* — Dominant competitors are very rare. Dominance often results from a quasi monopoly or from a strongly protected technological leadership.
- *"Strong* — Strong competitors can usually follow strategies of their choice, irrespective of their competitors' moves. Not all industries have dominant or strong competitors.
- *"Favorable* — When industries are fragmented, with no competitor clearly standing out, the leaders tend to be in a favorable position.
- *"Tenable* — A tenable position can usually be maintained profitably through specialization in a narrow or protected market niche. This can be a geographic specialization or a product specialization.
- *"Weak* — Weak competitors can be intrinsically too small to survive independently and profitably in the long term, given the competitive economics of their industry, or they can be larger and potentially stronger competitors, but suffering from costly past mistakes or from a critical weakness." (p.7)[13]

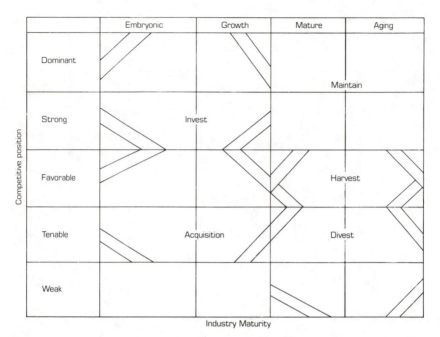

Figure 2.4   Industry Maturity — Competitive Position Matrix[13]
Reprinted with permission.

To practice such a strategy one needs to know the details about each major competitor, the rate of their progress, resource utilization, and market thrust. Such information is hard to get and, even if one gets it, the reliability is questionable. The resource deployment required could be substantial to thoroughly complete such an evaluation. This adds to the cost of developing new products and may ultimately defeat promising areas of growth. However, a general awareness of one's position in this matrix is critical. Often it is more cost-effective to use a consulting company. This provides the additional benefit of their experience base plus an unbiased opinion.

General Electric's Business Screen

GE recognized that the BCG growth/share matrix was too narrow to describe industry attractiveness by total market growth rate and business strength by market share. They felt that a number of other important variables should be included in the portfolio assessment of various businesses. Accordingly, GE asked McKinsey and Company to develop what is now known as *industry attractiveness/business strength matrix* as shown in Figure 2.5. The assessment requires the evaluation of both external and internal factors.

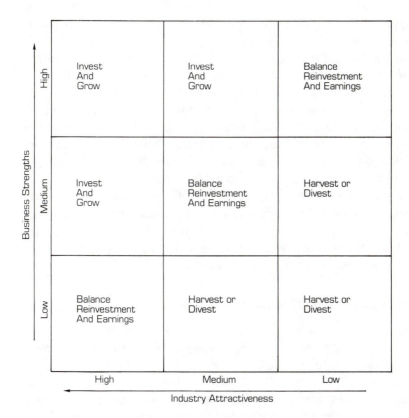

Figure 2.5   GE's Business Screen

The external factors are categorized into two major groups: micro factors and macro factors. Micro factors consider all the external variables that impact the industry such as, market size, market growth rate, competitive structure, industry profitability, barriers to entry, technology, etc. Macro factors consider the overall environment related to socio-economic and political climates of the region in which the business is conducted.

Critical internal factors which comprise a company's strengths include market share, marketing, R&D expenditure, customer service, raw material positioning, manufacturing, financial resources, breadth of product line, and managerial competence. The strength of these factors is evaluated vis-a-vis key competitors, resulting in an assessment of competitive position.

Each business is assessed on internal and external factors and assigned a position in a 3x3 matrix. The horizontal axis portrays industry attractiveness and the vertical axis competitive strength. Three categories (high, medium, and low) are used to classify both attractiveness and strength.

The position in the matrix provides a guide to possible strategic options such as: invest and grow; maintain selectively, ie, balance reinvestment and earnings; and harvest or divest.

The strategic formulation of each business is based on existing status and projected future. The existing status is evaluated based on historical and current data, whereas future status is based on forecasts. Based on this information, resource allocation is evaluated as to the viability and future profit potential of that business.

The actual methodology of using the GE screen requires that both internal and external factors be assigned a certain numerical weight to each variable depending upon its importance to the business. The cumulative number for business strength and industry attractiveness fixes the position of that business in the matrix.

Strategic Mission Determination

"The position of a business in a portfolio matrix does not determine its strategic mission — it only suggests alternatives and focuses attention on its future viability.

"Strategic missions are a link between portfolio strategy and individual businesses' strategies. They are not detailed strategy statements for the business, which include: a set of objectives, a definition of businesses in which SBUs compete, a basic competitive posture, a coherent set of functional policies, and priorities in resource allocation." (p.83)[2]

Strategic missions are a statement of objectives which make explicit the expected financial and market position trade-offs of a business. They include an accompanying statement of claims on corporate resources, thus providing a basis for discussion between the SBUs and the corporate parent. Irrespective of what portfolio approach is used, the task of defining a strategic mission remains the same. Nevertheless, the BCG growth share matrix is much more restrictive for such a definition than multi-factor criterion matrices.

The Attractiveness of Portfolio Planning Models

According to Haspeslagh, the portfolio planning models were designed to provide the following advantages.

- They provide managers a means to formulate a portfolio strategy for diversified industrial companies.

- They promote increased visibility of a business's strategic position through the definition of SBUs and portfolio matrix display.
- They provide a common basis such as cash flow to assess the trade off between short-term profits and market position.
- They provide an analytical framework for allocating resources directly and selectively.
- The methodology of portfolio planning should result in increased communication and strategic thinking across various organizational levels.
- They provide the potential to focus on a range of different issues, depending upon the economic environment. Issues such as a balanced cash flow are important in an environment of expensive capital, while strategic focus on competitive analysis rather than market analysis is more important in an environment of slow growth. (p.87)[2]

SUMMARY

The planning process evolved from basic financial planning consisting of a yearly operating budget for each business plus short term capital spending, to a plan based on future forecasts. The next step was externally focused planning oriented towards markets and competitors, which was followed by strategic evaluation of each business. These steps culminated in the business portfolio concept, where businesses are classified according to their potential for growth and cash generation, and resources are allocated and channelled from one business to another. The essential rationale of the business portfolio concept was to provide corporations with a balanced cash flow, by channelling cash from mature businesses to growth businesses and divesting the declining businesses.

The concept was backed with experience curve studies of product lines and businesses such as: automobiles, refrigerators, Japanese beer, chemicals, vacuum cleaners, and the Japanese motorcycle industry. In all cases, according to BCG, for every doubling in the number of units produced, the typical costs fell approximately 22 to 30 percent. Simplifying the application of experience curve to businesses with a number of product lines led to the development of BCG growth-share matrix.

In theory, the portfolio concepts made perfect sense and were adopted by a number of corporations. As these theories were put into practice, however, certain flaws emerged.

- The experience curve has a sound basis but its existence and impact is highly dependent upon the nature of products and markets. Extrapolation of the concept for formulating a strategy can often be misleading without examining the underlying assumptions.
- The time horizon for experience curve effects is highly variable and can vary from a few years to a few decades.
- The portfolio concepts when actually practiced created bureaucratic organizations, resulting from a force fit of concepts to real life situations.
- Portfolio concepts do not take into consideration factors which are important in the management and effective utilization of technology. In fact, technology development and deployment, critical to many industries, is not explicitly considered in the planning processes.
- The very concept of deemphasizing interdependicies has placed a very heavy financial burden on growth businesses, since it forces them to pay for all skills and talents required for business success. Yet most of these business units are incapable of utilizing those skills to the fullest. Further, it dilutes their effort from the main charter of their business by forcing them to manage functions in which they have no management competence.

In fact, the portfolio concepts are analytical tools, and their actual implementation without serious thought to their applicability and impact on various businesses and organizations is now perceived as an expensive experiment that often caused loss of competitive position and business failures.[14,15]

REFERENCES

1. Steiner, G.A. *Top Management Planning.* Macmillan, New York, 1969.
2. Haspeslagh, P.C.: Portfolio Planning Approaches and the Strategic Management Process in Diversified Industrial Companies. Ph.D. Thesis, Harvard Business School, 1983.
3. Verbal communication at Corporate Development Institute, March 3-4, 1986.
4. Porter, M.E.: Competitive Strategy: Techniques for Analyzing Industries and Competitors. The Free Press, New York, 1980.

5. Furrer, J.R.: Strategy Focus: The Customer or Competition. Conference Board Report No. 876, 1985, pp. 6-9.

6. Haspeslagh, P.C.: Ph.D. Thesis, pp. 538-539. Videotaped Interview with Reginal J. Jones, Harvard Business School, 1981.

7. Hall, W.K.: SBUs: Hot, New Topic in the Management of Diversification. *Business Horizons,* February, 1978.

8. Haspeslagh, P.C.: Ph.D. Thesis, Harvard Business School, pp. 72-73.

9. Henderson, B.D.: The Product Portfolio; The Boston Consulting Group Perspective No. 66, Boston, 1970.

10. Burnell, S.C.: The Ecology of Building, Harvesting and Holding Market Share. *Research in Marketing* 6: 1-63, 1983.

11. MacMillan, I.C., Hambrick, D.C., Day, D.L.: A Product Portfolio and Profitability - A PIMS Based Analysis Of Industrial Product Businesses. *Academy of Management Journal* 25: 733-755, 1982.

12. Zapp, G.M.: *The broader determinants of market strategy.* Conference Board Report No. 816, 1982, pp. 14-15.

13. Arthur D. Little: Strategic Management of Technology. *European Management Forum,* Davos, 1981.

14. Wheelwright, S.C.: Strategy, Management and Strategic Planning Approaches. *Interfaces* 14: 19-33, 1984.

15. Seegner, J.A.: Reversing the Images of BCG's Growth/Share Matrix. *Strategic Management Journal* 5: 93-97, 1984.

IMPACT OF STRATEGIC PLANNING AND IMPLEMENTATION ON CORPORATIONS

1 2 3 4 5 6 7 8 9 10

PORTFOLIO PLANNING MODELS AND STRATEGIC BUSINESS UNITS

The 1950s and 1960s was an era of unprecedent growth for U.S. corporations. This growth occurred by acquisitions and internal development of new products and processes, with little or no consideration given to the strategic fit of various businesses. This resulted in diversification with no strategic justification and loss of corporate influence over the various businesses. In the late 1960s and early 1970s the stringent government regulations for safety, environmental control, and energy-related projects forced corporations to commit large amounts of resources to various manufacturing facilities. This investment had little or no payback potential and impacted profits adversely. This was also an era of slow economic growth and emerging international competition. The result was flat or declining profits. In addition, a number of businesses became non-competitive due to cost components of product/service to various market segments, resulting from the lack of management attention.

The portfolio planning models provided management with strong tools to assess the profit potential of various businesses, a means of increasing corporate influence over businesses, and a promise of balanced cash flow. The implementation resulted in the formulation of strategic business units, evaluation of the businesses based on industry attractiveness and business strength, and assignment of a strategic mission to each SBU and allocating resources accordingly.

Portfolio planning concepts deemphasize management of interdependencies apart from cash across various businesses and provide no methodology for future growth. Portfolio concepts provide only one element of corporate strategy — the optimization of existing businesses for their profit potential. No consideration is given to the optimum utilization of human resources or the importance of technology apart from assigning this responsibility to the manager of the strategic business unit. In spite of the fact that portfolio concepts deemphasize interdependency and recommend each SBU to be autonomous and homogeneous, such is not the case in actual practice. There are a number of interdependencies such as engineering, safety, environment and health and a number of other functions which are centralized and serve a number of SBUs. The competence of these centralized functions plays an important role in the success or failure of SBUs. These functions are not the focal point in portfolio planning concepts and are generally ignored for their strategic importance, particularly in the development and deployment of technology.

It is not farfetched to say that portfolio planning models became corporate strategy and their implementation brought in a breed of management with little or no operating experience. These managers were mostly from corporate planning groups who understood only the theoretical aspects of portfolio planning.

THE IMPLEMENTATION OF PORTFOLIO PLANNING: ITS IMPACT ON CORPORATIONS

The overall result throughout corporate America was

1. Acquisitions and divestitures
2. Excellent cash position due to divestitures and depreciation
3. Vertical integration and horizontal diversification of product lines
4. Swing from commodity to specialty markets
5. Departure from high asset to relatively low asset business
6. Stock buy backs, lowered debt ratios, leveraged buy outs
7. Restructuring

The above actions are carried out through an organization structure which relies more on asset management than people management.

According to Paine Webber, the current restructuring of corporate America is pervasive and multifaceted. At least six major trends are reshaping the financial and organizational structure of U.S. corporations:

● "Consolidation of industries, both those in good financial health (media, food, financial services, regional banks) and those under financial pressure (oil, natural gas, airlines)

- "Leveraged buy outs of entire companies (Beatrice Companies, Inc.; R.H. Macy & Co., Inc.; ARA Inc.; Blue Bell Inc; Parsons Corporation; Levi Strauss & Co.; Wometco Broadcasting Co., Inc.)
- "Liquidating or streamlining of diversified companies by spinning off divisions via leveraged buy outs and sales to other corporations (ITT Corporation; Gulf & Western Industries, Inc.; City Investing Co.; RCA Corporation; American Can Company)
- "Hostile takeovers oriented toward dismembering the target (Revlon Inc.; Union Carbide Corporation; CBS Inc.; Walt Disney Productions; Crown Zellerbach Corporation; selected raids in the oil patch)
- "Major acquisitions, many designed to raise the acquirer's technological sophistication or alter its business mix (General Electric Co.-RCA; IBM-ROLM Corporation; General Motors-Electronic Data Systems Corporation; General Motors-Hughes Company, Inc.; Monsanto Company-G.D. Searle & Co.; United States Steel Corporation-Texas Oil & Gas Corporation; St. Regis-Champion International Corporation; acquisition of brokerage firms)
- "Heavy use of leverage and share repurchases to return capital to shareholders, raise earnings per share and discourage hostile tender offers."[1] *Reprinted with permission.*

The above actions are viewed as positive by the investment community, with the assumption that the restructuring will help maintain the profitability of corporations by redeploying people, capital, factories and natural resources. A further assumption is that the restructuring will do much to improve U.S. productivity which has steadily slowed for two decades and currently lags far behind that of Europe and Japan. These assumptions are perfectly valid on a short term basis. However, long-term results depend upon how well corporations handle the human element involved in restructuring and how well they manage the technology base which has been responsible for the U.S. strength throughout the twentieth century.

The analytical evaluation of various businesses within corporations led to classifying businesses for growth, harvesting, or divesting. The implementation of SBUs led to a bureaucratic organization where even segments of SBUs became independent entities leading to top-heavy organizations. These changes occurred over a period of years. The initial result of implementing portfolio concepts was a turnaround in the performance, which was a result of divestitures or shut down of nonprofitable facilities. The remaining businesses within the corporations consisted mostly of mature product lines which were being managed by top heavy management structures and were allocated resources far in excess to the industry attractiveness of these businesses. This became obvious as Western Europe, Japan, and newly developing countries were able to use standardized technologies and produce goods at a lower cost than U.S. corporations. The result was a loss of competitive position not only in the U.S., but in international markets as well.

A majority of diversified corporations employ portfolio planning concepts as a part of corporate strategy. The application of portfolio concepts could vary from using analytical aspects only to their full implementation. Portfolio planning techniques propagated the concept of resource allocation, depending upon industry attractiveness and business strength. To accomplish this the businesses had to be isolated on some rational basis. The division occurred based on one or more of the following factors.

1. End-use markets, eg, agricultural chemicals, pharmaceuticals, etc.
2. Commodity vs. specialty
3. Customer service intensity
4. Mature vs. growth
5. High tech vs. low tech
6. Degree of horizontal diversification
7. Degree of vertical integration.

The results were given the name of strategic business units, and their various segments were analyzed for cash flow, market share, growth rate, etc. using quantitative evaluation techniques. Each business was assigned a position in the portfolio grid or matrix. The position in the matrix provided options, resulting in businesses being labeled for harvesting or divesting, maintaining, and growth categories.

CHANGING BUSINESS ENVIRONMENT OF THE 1970s

The changing business environment of the 1970s and 1980s has revolutionized the structure of business in the United States. This has occurred due to social, political, economic and technological changes. The development and implementation of strategic business planning has resulted in the formulation of business units to be bought or sold, formed, dissolved, or redirected. Only top management has been permanent. Their emphasis has been on management of resources rather than ownership of assets. Value added at each level of management or operating unit has become a key criterion in the new structure of management. Advancements in communication technology and management systems have resulted in eliminating or reducing the middle management function. The new strategic hierarchy in diversified corporations has four levels of management: corporate, sector, group and strategic business unit. (pp.1–4)[2]

Corporate

The major strategic decisions at the corporate level are the selection of corporate mission and future direction regarding which businesses they will participate in, and the resource commitment to these businesses. Corporate hierarchy is essentially a complex of financial and management teams, with the main objectives of maximizing stockholders equities, formulating overall corporate objectives, balancing corporate business portfolios, assigning strategic missions to various SBUs, and generating strategic alternatives to the company as a whole. (p.4)[2]

Business Sectors

Most strategic planning takes place in the business sector, resulting in commitments regarding in which businesses a corporation wants to be involved and how to go about achieving this end, ie, acquisitions, joint ventures, deployment of venture capital, or internal development. These decisions are made based on available resources and competencies within the corporation. One key decision at this level is the choice of the appropriate strategic organization within the sector — the number and types of business units it will constitute, the basis for the formulation of strategic business units, their organization, and management of interdependencies. Sector management is a part of the corporate team. (p.5)[2]

Group Level

The group level is a loose link between corporate level and strategic business units. This level of management assures that strategic objectives of business units are being met and almost acts as a watchdog between strategic and operating control.

Strategic Business Units

The concept of strategic business units has been discussed in detail in Chapter 2. This is the lowest level where strategic planning is done based on the complexity of markets, products, and services. Their thrust is both strategic and operational. The major focus is on product/market segmentation, identification of future opportunities, formulating product strategies, and addressing tactical questions such as pricing, marketing policy, customer service, etc.

The formulation and implementation of this hierarchy of strategic management has provided corporations with a great deal of flexibility in dealing with SBUs on a decentralized differential management basis. Since the SBUs are self-contained units, the corporation has a great latitude in deciding the fate of the SBUs. Depending upon top management's assessment, these units can be expanded or contracted, closed down or divested. (p.6)[2]

It is too early to evaluate the long-term impact of this new strategic management style on employees' morale. The initial indications are that it has created a strong feeling of detachment between the corporation and its employees. The fear of an uncertain future and the lack of continuity is bound to adversely impact the creative and innovative processes within organizations — the two most important requirements for the long term viability of a successful company. Strategic business planning and implementation has created a paradoxical situation: it has provided top management tools to deal with existing problems of facing global competition, but its implementation has resulted in demoralization of employees, which is detrimental to future success, the very purpose of strategic planning. It is up to top management to assure that these two issues are dealt with during the planning process.

CASE HISTORIES

The impact of strategic planning and implementation is best explained by considering the case histories of three major companies: Allied Corporation, Monsanto Company and Minnesota Mining & Mfg. Company (3M). These three corporations were selected as examples due to the diversity of their products, markets, and their strategic thrust. The information was obtained from annual and 10K reports. Their operations from 1977–1984 were reviewed with emphasis placed on strategy, organization, and acquisition/ divestitures. Allied and Monsanto were included in Philippe's survey as the corporations that employ portfolio planning concepts, whereas 3M was not.

Allied Corporation

Allied Corporation (formerly Allied Chemical) is an international manufacturer of electronic equipment, a gas and oil producer, and a chemical manufacturer, with a total sales of about $10.7 billion per year.

Prior to 1979, Allied reported financial data for three broad operating segments, but was organized into six segments. Corporate goals or strategy was loosely defined as "identifying those (businesses) we want to stay with or expand and those we want to get out of." Criteria were listed as "problems of raw material supply or technology — environmental risks we don't feel justified in assuming." Using this strategy, Allied got out of the following businesses: PVC, melamine dinnerware, gasoline refining and retailing, pigments, arsenical insecticides, Kepone, and Mirex.

Under the direction of a new Chairman and CEO, Allied underwent a major reorganization in 1979. A corporate strategy was formulated having the following goals: 1) double earnings from continuing businesses within five years; 2) substantially improve pre-tax return on assets; and 3) improve liquidity and corporate balance sheet to upgrade credit rating.

A generalized plan to achieve these goals was also outlined as follows: 1) long-term program to diversify product lines; 2) sell unprofitable and marginally profitable businesses; 3) reorganize to lower overhead costs and achieve greater efficiency and management control; and 4) expansion of research and development program with special emphasis on turning laboratory discoveries into profitable new products.

From 1979 to 1982, this plan was implemented through an active acquisition and divestiture program as listed in Table 3.1. The acquisitions were in higher technology, higher value-added, and lower capital-intensive areas than had made up Allied businesses before. Divestitures were in areas with opposite characteristics.

Divestitures	Year	Acquisitions
• Phase out insecticides and herbicides	1975	
• Sold pigments and dye business	1976	
• Sold furnace coke plant	1977	
• Sold coal and coke business	1979	Bought Eltra Corp. electrical and industrial products company
• Sold smaller chemical business (i.e. $Cl_2/NaOH$, thermoset molding compounds and paving operations)	1980	Acquired 49% of Mexican Alum. producer Valley Mineral Products Corp. (steel making products and refractory Interest in Canadian Biologicals Interest in Calgene Inc. (both biotech)
• Sold 2 Canadian oil and gas subsidiaries		Bunker Ramo Corp. (electronics) 1981
• Closed nuclear fuel reprocessing plant		Fisher Scientific Corp. (instruments)
• Sold H_2SO_4 and toluene diisocyanate plants		Gyrex Corporation (electronics equipment)
• Sold Converse (athletic shoes)	1982	Bendix Corp. merger
• Sold Borg Textile (deep pile fabrics)		Martin Marietta Corp. Instrumentation Lab., (Biomedical instruments)
• Closed European auto seat belt business		Supron Energy Corp. (oil and gas) Nitragin Co. (genetic eng.)
• Sold liquid fertilizer operations	1983	Semi-Alloys Inc. (manufacturing) of components for semi-conductor applications

● Sold machine tool business (part of Bendix)	1984	Amex Systems, Inc
		Timex Corp. gyro business
		King Radio Corp. 50% interest in ENSTAR Corp. (Indonesian gas venture)
	1985	Allied-Signal merger

Potential Divestitures
● Prestolite Battery
● C&D Power Systems
● North American Refractories
● Some segments of Signal Cos.

Table 3.1   Acquisition & Divestiture Program: Allied Corporation

In 1982 Allied was approached by Bendix Corporation for a merger. Since such a transaction would enable Allied to achieve several of its strategic objectives, negotiations were entered into, and the merger was approved in 1983, resulting in a new organization consisting of five sectors.

In 1985, shareholders of Allied Corporation and the Signal Companies approved the $5 billion merger of the two companies into Allied-Signal Inc. This merger has resulted in another reorganization and restructuring and reduction in work force of thousands of employees.

As a result of mergers, acquisitions, and divestitures, Allied sales increased from $2.36 billion in 1977 to $10.7 billion in 1984, operating income increased from $324 million to $1.34 billion, and R&D expenses increased from $51 million to $312 million.

Monsanto Company

Monsanto Company is a multinational industrial company engaged primarily in the manufacture of chemicals. Other products include agricultural products, man-made fibers, electronics materials, industrial process controls, and other capital equipment.

Monsanto's organizational structure has not varied greatly from 1975 until 1984. In 1975, five operating companies and an international division made up the operating structure. Minor changes were made in 1979, when Fisher Controls was elevated to company status, and the chemical companies were realigned. The six operating companies were reorganized again in 1982 with only minor regrouping.

In 1985 Monsanto acquired G.D. Searle to provide a link between the newly developed products from life sciences research and the market place. To accommodate the acquisition, Monsanto went through a major restructuring including four major components: strengthening the company's position in a number of current and developmental programs; withdrawal from selected low return businesses and production facilities; the sale of certain assets that no longer have strategic importance; and a reduction in employment.

Reorganization will result in the following major business entities: the newly formed Monsanto Chemical Co. and Monsanto Agricultural Co., the existing G.D. Searle and Co., Fisher Controls International Inc., and Monsanto Electronic Materials Co. This restructuring will result in a reduction of thousands of employees.

The corporate goal established in 1972 was to double earnings every ten years. The goal was readjusted after three or four years to account for inflation, ie, doubling earning in real terms after accounting for inflation. Internal attainment of this goal was expected as illustrated by the following quote: "Most of Monsanto's growth for the 1980s is expected to come from existing businesses. New applications, new markets and new related products will help retain the vibrancy of established businesses." (p. 19)[3] Major areas stressed were: 1) new applications, new markets, and new related products for established businesses; 2) geographic expansion of existing product lines; 3) search for new growth opportunities outside current areas (acquisition); and 4) expectation of research and development (R&D) to be a major source of new businesses.

Through 1983, very little variation from this plan can be noticed. Major research and development (R&D) areas were shifted from the traditional businesses towards life sciences, biotechnology, electronics, and new materials.

Monsanto's acquisition and divestiture activities are shown in Table 3.2 and consist mainly of shedding unprofitable businesses and plants and acquiring high-tech companies.

In 1984, Monsanto's CEO of eleven years retired. Strategy statements by new management vary only slightly as illustrated by the following quote: "Monsanto's strategy is to expand towards production of higher value proprietary and specialty products." (p. 4)[4]

Elements of the strategy are listed by Monsanto to: 1) renew our core chemical businesses; 2) increase our options for growth; 3) em-

Divestitures	Year	Acquisitions
	1979	Bought Radiation Dynamics (manufacturer of electron-beam process equipment)
Closed European nylon operations	1979	Merged Fisher Controls with General Electric Co., Ltd, U.K. (valves and instruments
Sold polyester filament business	1980	
Sold Aiscondel, S.A. (Spanish plastic subsidiary)		
Sold J-V with Conoco (olefins and aromatics)	1981	Bought interest in Biogen (Swiss genetic engineering co.)
		Bought 30% of Colagen Corp. (proteins for human tissue repair)
		Acquired total owner- ship of Fisher Controls
		Bought soybean seed company, Hartz Seed
		Bought Continental Pharma S.A. (European pharmaceutical)
Sold European acrylic fibers business		Acquired sole ownership of Polyamide Intermediates Ltd. (nylon intermediates in U.K.)
Potential Divestitures		
Petro-Chemical Complex at Texas City, Texas	1984	Acquired Continental Pharma, S.A. (Belgium pharmaceutical)
Insecticide business (Parathion)	1985	Acquired G.D. Searle
Oil and gas division		
Consumer Products and Equal aspartame business.		
(from G.D. Searle Acquisition)		
Gradual withdrawal as a supplier of nylon yarns for apparel and hosiery.		

Table 3.2 Divestitures and Acquisitions: Monsanto Company

phasize growth around the world; 4) extend market leadership of our growth businesses; 5) create windows on new technology; and 6) anticipate and respond to society's expectations.

Monsanto has continued its corporate strategy and direction by building on its major interests in these broad business areas: life sciences, chemical sciences, and engineered materials and products. Each area has a different focus and emphasis. The life science efforts are being supported by extensive research in biotechnology. Emphasis for chemical sciences is on innovation, technology, customer service, and efficiency. Monsanto expects rapid growth from engineered materials and products through engineering, applications technology, high quality, and specialized skills to provide customer needs.

Monsanto's operating philosophy is to become "the best in what we do," and this was how they operated in 1984 and plan to in the future.

Research and Development efforts have been expanded to support the business direction, with a record spending level in 1984 and continued growth since 1982. In 1984, 47 percent of Monsanto's research and development expenses were in the life sciences area.

Monsanto's growth plans continue to be internally focused. While acquisitions are seen as a major future option, they will be used to extend existing product lines to complement internal growth. Their annual reports have consistently contained a review of external economic conditions and/or major markets. These items include consumer spending, new housing units, motor vehicle production, and corn acreages.

As a result of internal growth and with the acquisition of Fisher Controls, Monsanto sales increased from $4.59 billion in 1977 to $6.7 billion in 1984, operating income increased from $637 million to $677 million and research and development expenses increased from $132 million to $385 million.

3M Corporation

3M Corporation is an international manufacturer of a diverse line of industrial and consumer products. It is comprised of approximately 100 profit centers in 50 countries, each of which is charged with "meeting (their) minimum standards for growth and profitability through the introduction of new products and the development of new businesses." (cover page)[5] The company's sales growth is expected to come from: 1) new and improved products; 2) new applications for existing products; 3) new markets; 4) overseas economics; and 5) generally small and highly selective acquisitions.

3M also has a "grow and divide concept," such that when a business reaches a certain size it is divided into smaller units. The normal 3M progression is from project to department to full division status. 3M reports also stated in 1979 that each profit center has a "goal of generating 25 percent of sales from products introduced in the last five years." (p. 2)[6] An on-going goal, it was achieved again in 1984.

3M's basic organization did not vary much from 1977 to 1981; financial data was reported for nine product groups in 1977 and 1978. In 1979 a tenth group was added as a result of restructuring. After obtaining a new CEO in 1980, the product groups were consolidated under four business sectors but expanded to thirteen product groups.

Consistent with the reorganization of the product groups, 3M has three levels of research and development. The traditional *group (or division) laboratory* is responsible for serving the group's market needs and provides new products and process improvements for the group to serve customers effectively. The group laboratory typically addresses immediate and short-range needs of the product group. The *sector laboratory*'s role is developing and expanding a strong technology base in areas important to the sector's long-range direction. Its main thrust is to develop promising technologies so the sector has resources to produce new products over the intermediate term (5 to 10 years). *Central research* concentrates on long-range, pioneering programs. This research is aimed at finding new scientific information and developing new technologies that will help lead 3M into entirely new markets and businesses. The activities are generally focused on a time span of ten or more years into the future.

3Ms goals for growth and profitability were restated in 1982: 1) average sales growth of 10 percent per year after adjustment for inflation; 2) pre-tax profit margins of 20 percent or better; and 3) return on stockholders equity approaching 25 percent.

The following steps were taken or planned to achieve these goals: 1) restructuring into four business sectors based on related technologies; 2) a marketing program to increase cooperation and efficiency in sales organization; 3) additional emphasis on the highest possible quality products; and 4) more formal business planning.

Because of 3Ms emphasis on internal development of new products and businesses, their acquisition and divestiture activities have been rather limited. Three small acquisitions were reported and no divestitures were listed.

3M sales increased from $3.98 billion in 1977 to $7.7 billion in 1984, operating income increased from $794 million to $1.286 billion, and R&D expenses increased from $177 million to $443 million.

* * *

The evaluation of Allied, Monsanto, and 3M strategies indicates three distinctly different modes of operation. Most of Allied's growth has been through acquisition and mergers. How well the company will do in the future depends upon the extent to which new businesses and technologies can be integrated and the morale of the organization. As a general rule, when top management is busy with financial deals, it pays little attention to the organization; in addition, frequent acquisitions and divestitures tend to adversely impact the morale of the organization.

Monsanto has made a big commitment towards growth through technology. Its future success will depend upon how well technology is managed and integrated with business.

3M is a unique company because of its success in new product development, which is based on encouraging and assigning new product development responsibility to all the operating groups. Throughout the 1970s, 3M ignored the portfolio concept of strategic business planning, until it was formally introduced in 1981. Key elements of 3M strategic planning are: providing a better business unit description, a long range business plan to help innovators, and considering business strength as a key parameter in evaluating innovations.

IMPACT OF STRATEGIC PLANNING ON BUSINESSES

Irrespective of what mode of strategic planning is practiced or implemented, when the strategic planning process is misdirected, it adversely impacts both financial and human resources and can result in one or more of the following:

- Human and financial resources channelled towards unproductive targets.
- Acquisitions which become more of a liability rather than an opportunity for future growth.
- Divestitures of attractive and profitable businesses.
- Demoralization of the whole organization, which impacts the corporation's future viability.

In fact, the strategic business planning process did have an adverse impact on a large number of corporations, a fact well documented by practitioners and academics. The main reason for failure being the application of strategic business planning to the business environment of the 1970s and 1980s without giving sufficient thought to the long term concerns relating to technology and its impact on competitive position. The business environment of the 1960s, a period of high growth and stable markets, proved to be a fertile ground for propagating strategic business planning concepts based on growth rate and market share. During the unstable environment of the 1970s with high inflation, high interest rates and stiff government regulations, strategic business planning provided a means of balancing cash flow and determining relative resource deployment, but it did not address a methodology for staying competitive in a global environment. The quantitative nature of business planning overemphasized asset management rather than people management. The heavy emphasis on market share and growth rate also caused many corporations to acquire businesses which were perceived to be attractive based on strategic business planning principles, but were ultimately uneconomical. For example, Monsanto's entry into polyester based on the market for leisure suits proved to be an expensive mistake.[7]

Business Week attempted to evaluate the outcome of strategies followed by 33 different companies picked at random. The evaluation was a snapshot of how they were currently faring. Out of 33, 19 failed, ran into trouble or were abandoned, while only 14 could be deemed successful.[7]

Mergers and Acquisitions

In 1984, 2,543 deals were struck for $122 billion,[8] whereas in 1985 the dollar volume for mergers and acquisitions increased 47 percent to $179.6 billion for 3,001 deals.[9] While few analysts expect such a high level of acquisitions and mergers to continue indefinitely, this trend is expected to continue throughout the current decade. A number of reasons are cited for this activity level, varying from the influence of arbitragers and takeover artists such as Carl Icahn and T. Boone Pickens to the global competitive environment and increasing corporate thrust towards a more service oriented economy. Successful acquisitions and mergers took into consideration factors such as synergistic markets, technological fit, corporate culture, management competence and global competitive environment rather than financial considerations alone. Some examples of acquisitions which are considered to be successful include FMC's acquisition of Lithium Corporation of America, Standard Brand being acquired by Nabisco, Bendix and Allied merger and the acquisition of Weight Watchers by Heinz.[8]

"But the overall record of successful acquisitions and mergers is not encouraging. One out of three acquisitions is later undone. In the past five years the number of divestitures has jumped 35%, to 900, with a worth of $29.4 billion, as reported by T. Grimm & Co, the M&A specialists."[8]

In most mergers and acquisitions, the legal and financial components receive maximum attention and require a tremendous amount of time and effort from lawyers, investment bankers and busines managers — however an equally important part, which often controls the success or failure of the acquisition or merger, is organization and people related. In a study by Consultant Richard Boland, 50 chief executives were asked which of the 26 factors in an acquisition received maximum attention. Only 3 factors related to human resources were placed in the top 12 considerations (top management talent, depth of management talent and compatibility of organizational structure). In response to the question "given a second chance, what would be different in their evaluation," the same chief executives listed 7 organization and human factors among the top 12 considerations.[9] The "people trauma" of mergers has been well documented in an article dealing with the case histories of employees affected by acquisition and mergers.[10] It portrays their bitterness towards corporations manifested by low morale, no loyalty, and fear of job security. These factors contribute to low productivity, lack of motivation, and a hostile attitude. It is impossible for a corporation to be successful for any length of time when the employees have such negative attitudes.

Drawbacks

The strategic planning concepts and their impact on businesses as perceived by William J. Abernathy and Robert H. Hayes is stated in their article from *Harvard Business Review,* "These new [strategic] principles, despite their sophistication and wide-spread usefulness, encourage preference for (1) analytical detachment rather than insight that comes from 'hands on' experience, and (2) short term cost reduction rather than long term development of technological competitiveness. It is this new managerial gospel, we feel, that has played a major role in undermining the vigor of American Industry."[11]

A survey about planning systems and what is wrong with them, conducted by Gray, revealed that a majority of chief executives, corporate planning directors, and business unit heads attributed shortcomings to pre-implementing difficulties. Specifically these included:

1. "Poor preparation of line managers
2. "Faulty definition of business units
3. "Vaguely formulated goals
4. "Inadequate basis for action planning
5. "Badly handled reviews of business unit plans
6. "Inadequate linkage of strategic planning with other control systems." (p.91)[12]

To realize fully the impact of implementing strategic business planning from the late sixties until today, it is important to recognize that management structural changes also were occurring during this period. Top management's philosophy based on portfolio concepts was implemented throughout business segments. These actions generally were carried out by newly-minted middle management, who often had no consideration for the morale of the employees. This process occurred over a period of 15 years and had strong adverse impacts on technology in particular. The present trend of trying to develop morale with slogans and quick-fix strategies is totally unrealistic. Such a morale change must have top management's active involvement. If left to middle management alone, they are likely to go through the motions of doing so without accomplishing much, making the task all the more difficult.

Current Status and Future Implications

Today U.S. industry faces a strange dilemma: to survive, it has to become more competitive or else seek government protection. To become competitive, industry must reduce costs, improve product quality, and increase productivity of both blue and white collar workers. Productivity improvement requires employee motivation, multiple skill development, employer loyalty, and innovations in the manufacturing processes.

U.S. managers have chosen to reduce costs by decreasing capital deployment to maintain and enhance manufacturing facilities. This trend is well illustrated by Robert H. Hayes and Steven C. Wheelright in their book entitled *Restoring our Competitive Edge.*[13] The overall impact of U.S. managers' actions is summarized by Hayes and Wheelright as follows:

- "Financial considerations (and particularly short-term financial considerations based on such measures as ROI) have tended to dominate the thinking of U.S. managers much more than they have influenced the decisions of managers in other countries.
- "U.S. managers have been less sophisticated and imaginative in dealing with technological considerations than many of their international competitors. Instead many have focused their attention on financial and marketing issues.
- "U.S. managers have tended to separate complicated issues into simpler, specialized ones to a greater degree than their foreign counterparts. The objective of organizational design, of course, is to divide responsibilities in such a way that individuals have relatively simple tasks to perform. But these differentiated responsibilities must be pulled together by sophisticated, broadly gauged integrators who can deal with the total picture.
- "The U.S. penchant for separating and simplifying had led many American firms to diversify away from their core technologies and market to a much greater degree than do European or Japanese firms (or, indeed than do the most successful U.S. corporations).
- "Over the past 15 to 20 years a number of important U.S. manufacturing industries have competed primarily on dimensions of mass distribution, packaging, advertising, and the development of incremental new products to round out existing product lines or to attack specific market segments. They have not put effort into improving manufacturing capabilities.

"As a result, U.S. plants and equipment have been allowed to age. The country's technological advantage has been eroded by the decline in expenditures for new product R&D and for new processing technologies. The best managerial talent has been directed toward "fast tracks" that often ignored or excluded direct manufacturing experience. At the same time, promotions to top corporate positions increasingly have favored those who specialized in finance, marketing, accounting, or law.

"For years this aging of plants and equipment and the adoption of the fast track as the route to the top did not seem to impair the competitiveness of most U.S. manufacturing firms. Beginning in the 1970s, however, these companies suddenly found themselves pitted against those who did compete on such dimensions as defect-free-products, process innovation, and delivery dependability. Increasingly, they found themselves displaced, first in international markets and then in their home market. The recognition of their apparent vulnerability came as a shock to many American managers, who began to seek equally quick and dramatic "solutions" — especially those that were easy to copy, such as quality circles, governmental assistance, and robotics."[13] *Reprinted with permission.*

In addition to these actions, U.S. managers have chosen to reduce costs by early retirements and massive layoffs. Today's plight of U.S. industry is a result of 15 years of inefficient management due to a heavy reliance on strategic business planning tools and a lack of in depth knowledge about technology and markets. Even now the solutions being adopted are short term with little vision of the future.

Consider two of the major actions taken by industry to stay competitive:

- The reduction in capital investment has resulted in inefficient manufacturing facilities, causing poor product quality, high production costs, unsafe operations and environmentally unsound processes.
- Massive layoffs and early retirements have reduced costs but reflect little or no future planning. This point is illustrated in the *Business Week* article that speaks of "de-massing, downsizing and restructuring"[14], which means one and only one thing to millions of American workers — loss of job, self-esteem and future uncertainty. Such corporate actions have resulted in demoralizing the rest of the employees, who spend more time worrying about job security rather than being creative.

In order for the reduction of asset deployment and reduction in work force to produce long-term positive results, the capital investment must be well planned and judged not only on return on investment but also based on the organization's competency that is responsible for its deployment. More often than not, the investment looks attractive on paper but when actually deployed produces results far less reliable than predictions and in many cases is an outright waste. This occurs because of 1) technology management that is more involved in corporate politics than technology development; 2) interdepartmental friction; 3) inadequate process and product development; 4) low motivation and morale; and 5) lack of experienced people or plain apathy towards work.

The present corporate managements' actions of reducing costs by early retirements and massive layoffs, irrespective of skills and talents being lost, are only enhancing the above nonproductive traits. Little attempt has been made to reverse this trend through realistic planning, developing multiple employee skills, and building competencies or boosting morale and motivation within the organization. If the existing trend continues, the fate of a number of U.S. industries will be dependent upon government protection and will ultimately result in lower quality, more expensive products being produced and consumed in the United States. The overall result will be a lower standard of living or the transformation of U.S. industry into a satellite of Japanese investment and management.

Evidence of this scenario already exists. The Japanese have established production facilities for a number of U.S. industries such as automobile, steel, video recorders, compact discs, semiconductors, and telecommunications gear. All told, some 500 Japanese companies now manufacture or assemble in the U.S. At the end of 1985, Japanese investments in the United States were $19.1 billion, still far below investments of Britain or the Netherlands.[15] "The nature and growth rate of Japan's investment, however, is different. It has nearly tripled from 1980 to 1985, and Japan's Ministry of International Trade and Industry (MITI) expects the country's U.S. manufacturing investment to grow by 14.2 percent each year until 2000. That would be a tenfold increase over the early 1980s level, and now, because of the dramatic appreciation of the yen, even that forecast could be too low. MITI says Japanese investment will create 840 thousand more U.S. jobs by the century's end, and millions more will be created indirectly."[15]

What impact Japanese investment and management style will have on the U.S. is a matter of conjecture. The impact could vary from that of the nineteenth century colonial philosophies of the British, French and Dutch (using vast U.S. natural resources and improved technologies to capture world markets and U.S. citizens to provide semi-skilled labor) to exploiting synergistic effects of U.S. and Japanese talents and enhancing the living standard of both countries.

SUMMARY

Strategic business planning techniques have been in use for the last two decades. Detailed studies of their impact on businesses indicate the following drawbacks:

- Their quantitative nature hinders originality, a requirement for successful planning.
- The planning departments became too bureaucratic and unrealistic in setting their goals.
- The planning process and plans were forced upon other functions, which resulted in a lack of team spirit.
- Their organization resulted in diffused responsibilities for executing the plan.
- Planning was externally oriented; there was inadequate assessment of internal strengths and weaknesses.
- The thrust of planning was toward markets; there was little or no role for technology.

Strategic planning techniques and their implementation have had far reaching impacts both on business and technology. They have created a number of future challenges for the corporations which must be addressed, evaluated, planned for, and dealt with while keeping in mind the lessons learned from the past.

Neither strategic planning nor sophisticated techniques by themselves are sure-fire formulas for success. Nothing can substitute for first-hand knowledge of the businesses. Such knowledge combines internal and external business/technology factors with a strong commitment to succeed. This attitude requires participative management, a strong team spirit, and grassroot planning. These factors can then be enhanced by the use of strategic planning techniques.

REFERENCES

1. Paine Webber: Money Notes Part 2, April, 1986.

2. Royce, S.W., Mcleod, W.P.: Creating Flexibility for Corporate Structure, SRI Report 1054, 1980.

3. Monsanto Annual Report, 1979.

4. Monsanto Annual Report, 1983.

5. 3M Annual Report, 1985.

6. 3M Annual Report, 1979.

7. The New Breed of Strategic Planner. *Business Week,* Sept. 17, 1984, pp. 62–68.

8. Prosbesch, S.E.: Do mergers really work? *Business Week,* June 4, 1985, p. 88.

9. Kanter, R.M.: Management Review. American Management Association. October, 1986 pp. 16-17.

10. People Trauma. *The New York Times.* Nov. 19, 1985.

11. Hayes, H.R., Abernathy, J. W.: Managing Our Way to Economic Decline. *Harvard Business Review* 58:68, 1980.

12. Gray, H.D.: Uses and Misuses of Strategic Planning. *Harvard Business Review* 64:91, 1986.

13. Hayes, R.H., Wheelright, S. C.: *Restoring Our Competitive Edge — Competing Through Manufacturing.* John Wiley & Sons, New York, 1984, pp. 19–20.

14. Nussbaum, B., Failla, K., Eklund, C. S., et al: The End of Corporate Loyalty. *Business Week,* Aug. 4, 1986, pp. 42–43.

15. Holstein, W.J.: Japan, U.S.A. *Business Week,* July 14, 1986, p. 46.

SCIENCE/TECHNOLOGY — ITS IMPORTANCE, MANAGEMENT AND PHILOSOPHY

1234567890

IMPORTANCE OF SCIENCE/TECHNOLOGY

In 1984, the Conference Board conducted a survey entitled "The Impact of Technological Change on Corporate and R&D Management." This survey reflects the opinion of 232 executives in 15 highly industrialized nations: 189 U.S., 1 Japanese, and 42 European. The typical response of participants was that the relationship between technology and a company's competitive strength is gaining ever-widening recognition. "Technological innovation will dictate competitive advantage and disadvantage." This statement by a senior U.S. executive is typical of the responses received.[1] Similarly, a survey of European executives by Booz, Allen, and Hamilton, Inc., found that ". . .technology represents an opportunity, a threat, a tool — but not an end in itself yet its impact on competitive position — can be so profound that it must be thoroughly understood and managed, if unacceptable risks are not to be run."[2]

Responses to the Conference Board survey indicated a need for emphasis in the following technology related areas:

- "Greater involvement of technology managers in setting corporate direction
- "Increasing influence of technology on corporate strategy
- "Increasing formal technology forecasting
- "Improving the linkage of technology to other business functions
- "Raising the stature of technology management with respect to other functions
- "Increasing involvement of R&D people in the corporate planning process

- "Increasing involvement of the CEO in the technological planning process." (p.7)[1] *Reprinted with permission.*

The importance of research and development (R&D) in maintaining the U.S. lead in the global economy was emphasized by Ian M. Ross, President of AT&T Bell Laboratories who was a keynote speaker at a meeting in New York City, in his speech entitled "R&D: Key Issues for Management in 1986" sponsored by the Conference Board.[3] He stated "It's value-added that R&D brings to a nation's resources that determines its industrial competitiveness".[3] Ross suggests that 50 to 60 percent of economic growth can be attributed to technological innovations and the United States in particular must use technology to drive down the labor content of its products. He points out the differences in hourly labor costs which are $12.26 in the United States and $6.48 and $1.30 in Japan and Korea respectively. The need is to focus more R&D on process and manufacturing. "He believes that such an effort may correct the increasing failure of U.S. companies to move new products from design and manufacturing into the market place"[3] in a timely and efficient way.

Ross also emphasizes the importance of staying competitive in manufacturing industries, since it produces 85 percent of U.S. wealth. Further, he points out that the United States cannot be "indifferent to the strategic and economic benefits of a diversified industrial base."[3] It is a combination of high tech and manufacturing industries which is essential for the U.S. economic success, such as the use of computers and robots in the auto industry.

The same is true for other "low or medium range technology industries" such as steel, chemicals, and agricultural, where the use of high tech will have an elevating effect in raising the value of these industries and services.

Ross points out that the United States must excel in four basic industries. Computer and telecommunications are foremost because with "this base we can provide an almost infinite variety of services" through systems engineering. The U.S. must also keep its lead in aerospace and aviation since it has "many implications for our future and symbolizes new frontiers."[3]

Chemicals and pharmaceuticals are paramount, being "critical to the fundamentals of a nation's life - its food, health and material needs. Biotechnology, including instrumentation and equipment to apply it, is another front runner. R&D, however, has to be the foundation. Its creation, application and protection are keys to our overall success."[3]

In the same meeting Kenichi Ohmae, a Tokyo based managing director of McKinsey & Co., emphasized the importance of global markets, particularly United States, Japan and Europe. These three combined provide 600 million consumers and about $10,000 per capita in gross national product. Those three regions, Ohmae says, also make and consume 85 percent of all high technology goods.

The importance of technology is well recognized in the welfare of a nation's economy; thus, it is important to review what has happened to the management of technology since World War II and where it stands today, particularly in diversified industrial companies.

TECHNOLOGY MANAGEMENT/PHILOSOPHY

1945-1965

From 1945 to 1965, the management of science and technology was based on Vannevar Bush's philosophy,[4] which became popular as a result of President Roosevelt requesting Bush, who was Director of the Office of Scientific Research and Development, to draw upon his wartime experience and make recommendations on the following points:

- Use of technology developed during wartime for peaceful purposes
- Research programs in medicine
- Role of government to aid research activities by public and private organizations
- Programs for discovering and developing scientific talent in American youth.

Dr. Bush appointed four distinguished committees, which consisted of well known scientists and executives both from industry and academics. Each committee was assigned one major area. On July 5, 1945, a final report was submitted to President Roosevelt with a recommendation for the establishment of the National Science Foundation (NSF) whose purpose should be to "Develop and promote a national policy for scientific research and scientific education. . . ., support basic research in non-profit organizations. . ., develop scientific talent in American youth by means of scholarships and fellowships, and. . .support long range research on military matters."[4]

The legislation to create NSF was introduced in 1945, but the agency was not established until 1950. During that period the creation of the Atomic Energy Commission and scientific offices in each of the armed services largely answered defense related concerns, and the expansion of the National Institute of Health took the responsibility of medical research.

In addition to specific recommendations, the Bush report contained a number of statements which became almost a guiding philosophy in the management of research and technology in the United States until the mid 1960s. Some of the key statements are:

- "Basic research leads to new knowledge," Bush wrote. "It provides scientific capital. It creates the fund from which the practical applications of knowledge must be drawn. New products and new processes do not appear full grown. They are founded on new principles and new conceptions, which in turn are painstakingly developed by research in the purest realm of science."[4]

- "But without scientific progress no amount of achievement in other directions can insure our health, prosperity, and security as a nation in the modern world."[4]

- "New manufacturing industries can be started and many older industries greatly strengthened and expanded if we continue to study nature's laws and apply new knowledge to practical purpose.... But to achieve these objectives — to secure a high level of employment, to maintain a position of world leadership — the flow of new scientific knowledge must be both continuous and substantial."[4]

- "Scientific progress on a broad front results from the free play of free intellects, working on subjects of their own choice, in the manner dictated by their curiosity for exploration of the unknown."[4]

Science/Technology Push Model

Bush's views formed the basis of R&D for the next two decades and is shown by the following model (Fig. 4.1)

This theory, known as "science or technology push," dictates that innovations are an outcome of basic research.

Project Hindsight/Traces

Studies were undertaken by the Department of Defense to evaluate the usefulness of basic and goal-oriented research to innovations.

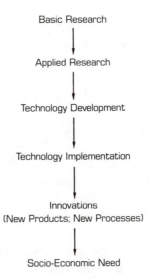

Figure 4.1   Science/Technology Push Model

These studies were given the name — Project Hindsight and TRACES.

During the mid 1960s the Department of Defense (DoD) instituted what was called "Project Hindsight" to assess relative contributions of science and technology to the development of 20 weapon systems which included the Polaris missile, the Minutemen ICBM and the C-141 aircraft.

This study was undertaken by DoD scientists and engineers to identify the factors underlying successful R&D programs. The objective of this study was to improve DoD resource allocation and program management procedures. The issues considered were: optimum balance between basic and applied research and effectiveness of R&D between DoD laboratories, industry and universities. (p.16)[5] An attempt was also made to determine the cost effectiveness of improving older weapon systems versus DoD investment in R&D.

Various weapon systems were divided into their constituent components. Each component was examined to assess contributions made by science or technology in increasing the performance or cost effectiveness compared to older systems. "Each discrete contribution was termed as an event. They were classified as either 'science events' if they stemmed from pure research or 'technology' events if they arose from mission-oriented research and resulted in a new or improved technique." (p.17)[5]

"The analysis of 20 weapon systems yielded nearly 700 distinct research and exploratory development events of which only 8 percent were found to be "science events" compared with 92 percent "technology events." (p.17)[5] The results of this study were questionable, since the work was undertaken by the DoD staff for the evaluation of its own operation, hence a built-in bias towards mission oriented research.[6]

In 1966 NSF invited proposals for a study to investigate the manner in which non-mission related research has contributed over a number of years to practical innovations of economic or social importance. In 1967 the Illinois Institute of Technology (IIT) was commissioned to carry out this study. IIT completed this report by the end of 1968, entitled "Technology in Retrospect and Critical Events in Science" which was given the acronym "TRACES."[7]

The approach taken was the same as project Hindsight, involving critical events leading to these five successful innovations: 1) magnetic ferrites; 2) the video tape recorder; 3) the oral contraceptive pill; 4) the electron microscope; and 5) matrix isolation.

The research events identified by the IIT team were classified into three categories.

1.   Pure research or basic research
2.   Mission oriented or applied research
3.   Development and applications (p.20)[5]

A total of 340 events were identified, 70 percent of which were the product of pure research, 20 percent of applied or mission oriented research and 10 percent of development and applications.

These findings were the reverse of the DoD study, and the difference was attributed to the time horizon over which the occurrence of events were looked at. The DoD study considered the past 20 years, whereas TRACES considered the past 30 years. It was identified that events which resulted from pure science took 20 to 30 years before they resulted in major innovations for socio-economic benefit. TRACES was criticized particularly on the grounds that the sample of five innovations studied was not entirely representative.

To eliminate doubts, NSF commissioned the Battelle Columbus Division to conduct further studies, ie, an extension of TRACES. In addition Battelle was asked if innovation could be managed.

Completed in 1973, the Battelle study[8] traced the main research and development events leading to eight major innovations: 1) the heart pace maker; 2) the hybrid grain associated with "green revolution"; 3) electrophotography; 4) input-output economic analysis; 5) organophosphorous insecticides; 6) oral contraceptives; 7) magnetic ferrites; and 8) video tape recorders. For comparison, three of the innovations considered previously were included. (p.21)[5]

The study differed from previous ones in pinpointing events which were critical to innovation, ie, without which innovation could not have occurred. Results indicated that 15 percent of the events were associated with pure research, 45 percent with applied research, and 40 percent with development work.

As to the question if innovations can be managed, the key factors identified were recognition of technical opportunity, recognition of need, and good internal R&D management.

The results of these studies indicate that neither basic science nor applied science and technology alone adequately describe the successful innovation process. It is a combination of a number of factors which interact and intermesh to produce successful results, and any simplistic model is likely to be misleading. However, it is important to realize that all the steps described in "Science/Technology Push" model are a must for successful innovations. A debate as to which factors are more important than the others is futile since a strong emphasis in one area will not compensate the weakness or need of other areas; hence, a balanced approach is needed.

It seems that little thought was given to time frame factors before instituting project Hindsight or TRACES. The main purpose of these projects was to evaluate federal funding or resource allocation to basic and applied research. Basic research has been responsible for major breakthroughs in science. Such breakthroughs are not a routine phenomenon, and it takes decades of work if not longer. Major scientific breakthroughs act as a sprouting point for building a reservoir of knowledge, which continues to expand as a result of more work in that area. This knowledge is drawn upon for a number of successful innovations.

Market Pull Model

During the 1960s, an alternative model of innovation began to become popular, particularly among economists. According to this model, innovations are an outcome of demands generated by market forces which arise from socio-economic needs. The recognition of these needs force technological innovations which draw upon applied and basic science to create the hardware which ultimately fulfills the socio- economic need. This model was given the name "Market Pull" and is described in Fig. 4.2

Figure 4.2   The Market Pull Model

The "Market Pull" model has very different implications from "Technology Push" model, particularly in the management and funding of science and technology. Innovations are an outcome of interactions between market needs and basic research; the steps in between ie, applied research, technology development, and implementation fill in the gap. For successful results, each component must be developed and aligned with the others in a fashion unique to each innovation. In addition, these components are not discrete steps; rather they overlap, and the line of demarcation where one begins and the other ends is thin at best.

During the late 1960s while federal agencies were studying how to allocate their resources for optimum utilization between basic science and technology, industry was going through a major transition. Recession and market dynamics forced business management to evaluate their central research philosophy. It was found that the resource allocation for central research was far in excess of its impact on profits. The majority of these organizations were soon dissolved and resources deployed elsewhere.

As pointed out in Chapter 2, the diversified corporations have three major elements of corporate strategy: portfolio planning, management of interdependencies, and future growth. In accordance with the portfolio planning philosophy, technology was aligned to different strategic business units, with parts of it such as engineering, environmental department, etc. managed as interdependencies under corporate management. Since the strategic business units are not homogeneous, in many cases technology responsibilities were further subdivided into strategic segments.

Little or no attention was paid to the strategic management of technology. The portfolio concepts provided a strong focus in the strategic management of businesses by creating SBUs but fell short of recognizing that technology segmentation does not follow the same rationale as the creation of an SBU. Technology development goes through a number of stages, each stage requiring special skills and talents. In addition there is a strong synergistic effect between different technology functions and even an overlap as the effort moves from laboratory to commercialization. It is not economically feasible to staff each SBU with all the skills and talents required to accomplish different innovations.

1970s

In the 1970s after dissolving central research and aligning technology to SBUs, a heavy emphasis was placed on externally driven tactical projects such as: 1) environmental problems; 2) cost reduction; 3) energy utilization; 4) product modification; 5) automation and optimization of manufacturing facilities for better process control, raw material efficiency, and safety; 6) raw material resourcing; and 7) creation of centralized safety, health, and toxicology groups.

Most of the technical effort in the industrial sector was focused in two areas:

- Environmental/safety legislation resulted in heavy emphasis being placed on: 1) the cleanup of air/water discharge from existing plants, and 2) improvement of plant sites to reduce worker exposure to potential hazards.
- Escalating oil/gas prices promoted the reduction of energy use or switch to cheaper sources.

This new focus had several implications.

- Lack of innovation. Very few significant technological breakthroughs occurred. When they did, few resources were dedicated to developing them.

Result: Fewer new technologies were commercially available for application in the early 1980s. Those technologies that are emerging will require another 3 to 5 years for full development.

- Foreign countries (ie, Japan) were continuing to identify and develop new technology. While U.S. industry was cleaning up existing plants, the Japanese were expanding their technology base. They also did a better job of recognizing market need (ie, electronics/automobiles) and addressing it with new innovative products.

  Result: U.S. industry entered the 1980s flat, while foreign competition entered in high speed. This, combined with a strong dollar has weakened U.S. trade position, which traditionally has been very strong.

- In the U.S. industrial sector, knowledge of and ability to serve markets has stagnated. All new technical people were brought into industry to meet environmental/energy needs. This means applying existing technology to existing plants, and requires little creativity. Their perception of industry was completely different than a technologist's in the 1950s and 1960s.

  Result: Innovation and creativity were not encouraged. Product lines stagnated because of a lack of market attention. The innovative, market oriented technologists required for the eighties had not been properly trained in the seventies.

- Complying with environmental regulations and reducing energy costs required a completely different management personality than is needed today. The type of manager bred in the 1970s is having a difficult time coping with the rapidly changing environment of the 1980s, where an in-depth knowledge of the markets/technology/manufacturing for each business unit is required.

  Result: Innovation/competitiveness in management was neither encouraged nor rewarded. Only obvious business decisions are made, with heavy emphasis on the use of consultants and a follow-the-leader approach. Foresight and entrepreneurial skills are lacking.

1980s

Industry has responded to the dynamic business conditions in the early 1980s by 1) focusing on cost reduction/productivity improvement through manpower reduction; 2) focusing on the short term (6 to 12 months), since the business environment is changing too fast to look beyond; 3) following the lead of other companies or management consultants in business decision making; and 4) growing through acquisition instead of technical development.

This response has led to the following problems. There is a danger of losing the remaining technology base, which is required to stay competitive in world markets. Industry has developed risk aversion in implementing the wealth of emerging technologies to upgrade existing businesses (materials/biotech/artificial intelligence/separation techniques/etc.). There is a lack of broad insight into customer technology/needs with no structure to develop it. The focus is again on the symptoms of the problem (ie, day-to-day management to maximize cash) rather than long term solutions. Management ranks are filled with managers (instead of leaders and entrepreneurs), inbred from the 1970s. Technical ranks are lacking direction. A lack of independence, creativity and market exposure was inbred from the 1970s. A reward system that is focused on short-term results, which ultimately will run our businesses (long term) into the ground.

These problems have resulted because industry did not include technology planning in its approach except for the small amount indicated in strategic business methodology. Top technology management was sent to various business schools for a period varying from two weeks to three months. Such training was supposed to educate them in business concepts and result in an integration of technology and business. It is important to recognize that top technology management was trained under the Bush philosophy and in the majority of cases they are an outcome of central research. In a fast changing business environment, where divestitures, acquisitions, and mergers have played a major roll, top management's attention to technology has been minimal apart from appropriating funds and delegating it to SBU managers. The very reason for the failure of a number of businesses has been lack of technology innovations both in process and product areas. The newly acquired businesses will face the same fate as declining businesses of today if inadequate attention is paid to their technologies.

The fate of technology in implementing portfolio concepts is well described by an analogy of a healthy person being physically split into different parts of the body, each part of the body being assigned to a different SBU, with growth businesses getting two or three parts. This type of split has resulted in decapitating the technology effort. The overall result has been an increase in technology budgets with a minimal impact on strengthening the competitive position of businesses.

LESSONS LEARNED FROM THE PAST

Since the 1960s, the business planning process has gone through four major changes; however none of these concepts takes into consideration the role of technology on businesses. The result is that technology planning has been static with the exception of management changes; technology has become reactive and looks for direction from businesses who in turn seek direction from business consulting firms; acquisitions and mergers have further diluted top management attention to technology, which was inadequate in the first place; and business management has lost perspective in recognizing what it takes to keep the technical community stimulated.

In many ways the sad plight of corporations today is the result of a general technology failure, which manifests itself by new processes not being effectively competitive because of cost curve position of markets served; existing technologies falling behind state of the art and having an adverse impact on the cost/price/performance of product lines; cost reduction and capacity expansion programs that are insufficient to deliver competitive advantage; major snags occurring in the development and commercialization of new products; and safety and environmental factors becoming a major issue.

The inefficiencies and failures of the technology function occurred and will continue to occur as long as the following factors are not recognized and corrected by top management:

- Lack of understanding between technologists and businessmen as to the role of technology in strategic business planning
- Assumption that technology can be managed based on strategic business planning concepts
- An attempt to force-fit business and technology rather then integrate it
- A lack of technical planning resulting in staffing fluctuations with the business cycle

The integration of business and technology is critical to success in today's environment of stiff competition, changing social values, and fast development of new technologies. Success in integrating these functions will depend on a corporation's ability to:

- Create a mutual understanding between business and technology, recognizing each other's needs and constraints
- Recognize the limitations of strategic business planning process
- Incorporate technology as a part of corporate strategic planning process
- Recognize that the effective utilization of human resources may be the only strategic advantage of a business or corporation.

Attempts to integrate business and technology will be challenging since no ready-made solutions exist. These concepts are neither taught in business schools nor addressed by management consultants. This unique challenge cannot be solved by divestitures, acquisitions, or cost control.

The challenge is to motivate technologists. This can best be accomplished by providing realistic challenge, direction, and an open environment with strong technology leadership. To bring about such a change, the presidents and CEOs of the corporations must show the same zeal for technology as they do for financial performance and be willing to take on the task themselves rather than delegate it. Their future financial performance will likely depend upon how well they handle this challenge.

FUTURE CHALLENGES

In the last decade, many corporations have been quite successful in handling a number of strategic surprises — stiff government regulations; maturing markets; and strong competition from Europe, Japan, and newly developing countries. The competing countries had taken advantage of basic U.S. technology and further enhanced it before building their manufacturing facilities, which provided them with improved and newer plants. In the United States, both business and technology performed admirably in meeting those challenges. But a price was paid: a constant redeployment of technologists without providing adequate training and a strong pressure on management to deploy both human and financial resources in facing the changing business environment. Such constant pressures led to inefficient use of resources and resulted in a trend of building bureaucratic and inefficient organizations. Corporations are now challenged to correct these inefficiencies.

The future survival of corporations depends on fresh and innovative approaches to define and meet business objectives. To do so successfully, technologists and businessmen must use the lessons learned during the past two decades to face the future. Specifically, they must understand that:

- Strategic planning is an excellent technique and, as with any other skill, it has its own experience curve and areas of application. The cumulative knowledge gained during the past 15 years should continue to be developed and deployed rather than condemned for its mistakes and short-sightedness.

- The inefficiencies and inertia of the existing organization must be corrected. The competitive forces of the future will have no tolerance for an inefficient operation and will demand a fast and successful implementation of technology and business to provide goods and services.

- The humane issue of retraining and redeployment of professionals is an organization's moral and ethical responsibility, but the individuals concerned must be receptive, not bitter. This issue has a great impact on the morale of the whole organization, hence, this area needs top management attention rather than delegation to lower level staff functions.

- Human resources can be redeployed and retrained at a far faster pace than was normally believed. To do so, however, certain key elements must exist, namely challenge, direction, and means. As individuals progress in their retraining, personal satisfaction and recognition by the organization and by peers provide further incentive. It is a well-recognized fact that people perform at their peak when challenged rather than when involved in routine tasks.

The new era of intense competition demands an organization staffed with multiskilled employees. More effective use of manpower occurs when each individual can perform diverse tasks, as opposed to the traditional reliance on a stable of specialists. These specialists are still critical to an organization, but the extent of their utilization will be less. Advances in communication technologies make this trend all the more inevitable, as the time spent in accessing and transferring information diminishes.

Successful retraining and redeployment requires a move away from traditional attitudes of staffing, where the categorization of functions led to rigid disciplines dictating who did what, allowing for little flexibility. In addition, successful retraining requires a recognition that most people have potential and desire to undertake new and diverse tasks. To implement this approach the organization must have: tolerance, open communications, leadership rather than bureaucratic management, and realistic planning and plans. The challenge is to integrate different skills, talents, and technologies which together result in a corporation being able to do a lot more with the same human and financial resources than the competition.

In the future, successful corporations will use concepts of participative management and multiple skill development, emphasize the importance of well defined objectives and direction, and provide an environment for the effective utilization of technology. These, together with strong leadership, will generate creative and innovative approaches and solutions to business/technology problems. They will make use of planning techniques developed in the past, but will diverge from past practices in that such techniques will be employed throughout the organization rather than by planners or top management alone.

SUMMARY

After World War II, when Europe was struggling to rebuild its economy, a large number of scientists and technologists emigrated to the United States. In addition, a number of technologies developed in Europe were made available to U.S. industry. A strong thrust in technology development, encouraged by President Roosevelt, was accelerated by immigrated talents and European technologies. The result was a tremendous number of technological innovations in the 1950s and 1960s. As Europe advanced towards economic recovery, the number of trained scientists and technologists emigrating to the United States decreased considerably.

At this same time, technology planning and management in the United States was synonymous with R&D based on Bush's philosophy that "scientific progress on a broad front results from the free play of free intellects, working on subjects of their own choice, in the manner dictated by their curiosity for explanation of unknown."[4] This was widely known as the science or technology push model. During the mid-1960s to 1970, corporations recognized that science or technology by itself has only a limited usefulness. The emergence of the "market pull" model raised serious questions about the resources committed to central research compared to their contribution to a corporation's profits. This evaluation led to the dissolution of most of the central research organizations. The gap created by both of these developments — the decline of European scientists and technologists emigrating to the United States and the dissolution of most corporations' central research organizations — has neither been recognized nor filled by industry.

A major limitation on training professionals in multiple disciplines was the mountainous task of obtaining and assimilating past information. With advances in computer sciences that task has decreased considerably. Such being the case, individuals are capable of working and acquiring a knowledge base in a larger number of fields than before. However, to take advantage of these advances in science, a concentrated effort has to be made by industry and academics in training scientists and technologists of the future.

Some of the important observations which enhance the management and interface between business people and technologists are:

- Realistic strategic planning — recognizing its strengths and weaknesses, particularly on human resource utilization.
- Incorporation of technology plan into business plan.
- Promotion of top level management from within a business. Advantages are experience and dedication to seeing that business succeeds long term.
- Overhaul of the management reward system to emphasize long-term results.
- Encourage multiple skill development using communication technology.
- More frequent movement of technologists between businesses (cross fertilization).
- Less frequent movement of business management to encourage longer term focus, to minimize time spent learning business, and maximize time spent running business.

REFERENCES

1. Brown, K.J.: The Impact of Technological Change on Corporate and R&D Management. The Conference Board; Report No. 170, 1984.
2. Booz, Allen and Hamilton, Inc.: *Management of Technology: A Survey of European Chief Executives.* 1984, p. 1.

3. Spalding, B.J.: A world future for R&D. *Chemical Week*, Feb. 26, 1986, pp. 15, 17.

4. Bush V.: Science - The Endless Frontier, July 1945, Reprinted by Armo Press, New York, 1980.

5. Irvine, J.; Martin, B.R.: Foresight in Science. Frances Pinter, Dover, N.H.

6. Sherwin, C.W., Isenson, R.S.: First Interim Report on Project Hindsight (Summary). Washington, D.C., Office of the Director of Defense Research and Engineering, 1966.

7. ITT Research Institute: Technology in Retrospect and Critical Events in Science. National Science Foundation, Washington, D.C., 1968.

8. Battelle Memorial Institute: Interactions of Science and Technology in the Innovation Process: Some Case Studies. Final Report Prepared for NSF, Battelle Columbus Laboratories, Columbus, Ohio, 1973.

KEY CONSIDERATIONS IN THE MANAGEMENT OF TECHNOLOGY

1 2 3 4 5 6 7 8 9 10

THE IMPACT OF TECHNOLOGY ON BUSINESS

Most industrial corporations spend 40 to 70 percent of their pretax income on technology.[1] This translates into the allocation of large capital expenditures and human resources towards maintaining, enhancing, and changing the direction of the businesses. Although technology plays such a major role in a corporation's performance, inadequate attention is paid to its planning and management. In the current state of planning, the major corporate emphasis is on marketing and financial issues, reflecting short-term financial results, micro-issues, and short-term resource allocation and funding.

The position of marketing as a dominant function of business has evolved from the concept that a good marketing department can overcome all the business hurdles. This was the case after World War II, when there was an abundance of demand and few competitors. The marketing department was the key to full participation in this boom. Although the role of marketing is still important, the modern environment of vigorous competition, customer sophistication, and quickly advancing technologies emphasize the need for additional talents in order to remain competitive in the market place. To market a product it must be cost competitive, cost effective, and equal or better in quality and service than what the competition can provide.

It is now technological attributes, which play an important role in present and future cost and quality of the product, that have become a dominant criterion in product saleability. Heavy emphasis on marketing alone is not likely to keep a business successful. A combination of both technical and market factors now controls the fate of a product line. Since these two functions form the heart of a business, their planning must be done in conjunction with each other, including inputs from both and resulting in an integrated technology/business plan.

Successful integration of technology and business planning can:

- Utilize technology-based resources to create an overall business edge.
- Recognize threats, needs, and opportunities to product lines from the technology standpoint and integrate those with the business plan.
- Develop products and new applications ahead of competition in areas identified by integrated technology/business plan.

Business plans deemphasize or ignore macro shifts in technology, the time span of major technological developments, and their impact on business.[2-6] Historically, business professionals with foresight were capable of comprehending and dealing with both issues. Examples of such individuals include the founders of many of the major corporations such as Johnson & Johnson Co., Minnesota Mining & Manufacturing Co., International Business Machines Corporation, Ford Motor Co., and ITT Corporation. Visualizing those individuals in today's environment of fierce competition and macro factors makes it clear that more than foresight is needed now. An example is the high tech industry's frequent pattern of initial success followed by failure. Success occurred due to individuals' foresight; failure resulted as the business grew in magnitude without an integration of business and technology. Failures arise in two ways, either by great foresight and entrepreneurial spirit that cannot develop the discipline needed to manage a growing business or by failure of the vision as routine takes over. These traits have been illustrated through the work of three entrepreneurs: Steven P. Jobs, Donald C. Burr and Mitchell D. Kapor, and their companies. Jobs started Apple Computer Inc. and built it from a garage operation into a billion-dollar business. Burr perceived the broad implications of airline deregulation and built a new customer base with no-frills fares, while inspiring his followers at People Express, Inc., with rhetoric and profit sharing. Kapor made Lotus Development Corporation into a model of organized creativity as well as a powerful contender in the software business. Each of these businesses face new challenges as the organizations have grown to thousands of employees and the creative energy of one individual is no longer sufficient to manage the business.[7]

"The entrepreneur brings creativity and inspiring leadership to new markets and opportunities."[7] But with time, "markets mature and become less forgiving, competition heightens, and the business cycle exacts its costs."[7] A company with thousands of employees and diverse markets is different from a newly started company in almost every respect. To stay successful, these companies need competent managers and farsighted administrators — the exact qualities that entrepreneurs lack or fail to develop within their organizations.

The concepts and methodology of technology planning are very similar to those of business planning. The inputs, implementation, management, time horizon, and uncertainty are vastly different. The critical success factor over the long term is to integrate business and technology planning into one overall plan.

KEY PREMISES

The recognition of certain key premises is essential in order to integrate technology and business together into a unified plan. These premises detail the concerns of technology planning that are different from business planning; although they have certain similarities, other concepts are radically different. Most of these premises have been discussed in the literature in context with managing technologies or technologists but have never been considered collectively to formulate a scheme of planning technology as a part of the business.

Technology planning is based on the following key premises.

- Technology is an integral part of businesses and its planning.
- Key technologies require at least an 8 to 15 year time frame to develop. The time horizon of technology planning is significantly longer than that of business.[8]
- Technology development goes through multiple stages, each stage requiring different skills and talents.
- Technology builds on prior technology and science builds on prior science, except for rare random discoveries.[9]
- Technology forecasting is a viable concept.[10]
- The behavior traits of technologists are different from those of businessmen.[9,11]

SCIENCE/TECHNOLOGY DEVELOPMENT AND IMPLEMENTATION

Science is an activity or process of generating knowledge over a long period of time. Thus, "science can be represented as a stream of events over time cumulating in a body of knowledge." (p.49)[9] The basic work in science is mostly carried out at the universities and certain government funded laboratories. These studies have no boundaries of containment and their fundamental purpose is to enhance the field of science beyond its existing boundaries. An example of such an effort is a Ph.D. thesis or postdoctoral work.

Applied science is directed toward developing and harnessing basic science to solve society's needs. Examples of such an effort are the development of new drugs, new pesticides, and new materials of construction such as high tech ceramics and composites.

According to Thomas J. Allen two other fields of human activity operate parallel to science and function both as contributors to scientific development and as beneficiaries of scientific accomplishment. The first activity is called technology development. This is a stream of knowledge translated into physical "hardware," which will eventually meet with some human use.[9] The second, technology implementation, is a much more general form of combined activity in which the ideas of science and the hardware of technology are actually put to some use in the socio-economic world environment. (p.49)[9]

Technology implementation addresses the actual question of producing products or services for consumption by society, while taking into consideration costs, safety, toxicity, and impact on the environment. The problems encountered in doing so are referred back to basic technology which draws upon applied and basic science for solution. Thus, the technologies continue to advance with time as more and more knowledge is developed in the fields they draw upon.

The activities of technology and its implementation, "while at various times in concert with science, have developed for the most part independently." (p.49)[9] Scientific knowledge is developed in discrete steps and can be visualized as a pyramid, starting from a point indicated by a major discovery and expanding into a full body of knowledge. Once a fundamental discovery is made, the subsequent knowledge-gaining process occurs at numerous places throughout the world and is communicated through scientific journals and professional meetings. The cumulative effect is furtherance of knowledge in the field of discovery and its subbranching in several other areas. Such is the case of atomic research after World War II leading to the development of a comprehensive knowledge base in nuclear science. Thus, the growth of knowledge in science is a systematic process of building knowledge based on previous knowledge. Technology developments occur to satisfy the needs of society using knowledge from basic and applied science to develop the appropriate hardware. Implementation employs a number of different technologies resulting in satisfying a particular need. The technology developments could be independent of each other, but combine at a later stage to serve a particular purpose. Each technology development is an outcome of a series of improvements in the development of hardware as the state of art progresses. By following the progress in science and technology, it is possible to visualize various opportunities and threats that might have an impact on the future of various businesses.

Figure 5.1 shows the interaction of basic and applied research through technology development, implementation and enhance-

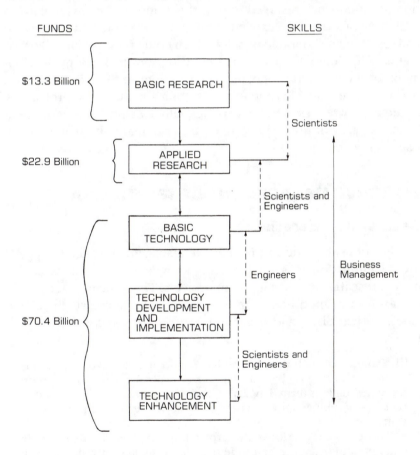

Figure 5.1   Stages of Technology Development 1985 U.S. R&D Funding

Source[12]	$(Billions)
Industry	53.2
Federal Government	49.8
Universities and Non-profit Organizations	3.6

ment, and the magnitude of funds allocated in each area along with skills at different stages of development. The key to successful and cost effective technology development is to have a mixture of the right skills and talents at different stages and encourage multiple skill development among different disciplines.

Multiple skill development makes it easier to move basic research through applied research and technology development to the market place at a pace faster than the routine procedure of each discipline being responsible only for what it does.

The ultimate result of applied science is technology implementation. Problems not resolved during this transfer of knowledge from each previous stage are carried through to the implementation stage and result in an economic penalty which could be substantial. For example, selection of the wrong materials or poor technology development for a manufacturing plant could amount to the loss of millions of dollars and valuable time in penetrating a market. The probability of such occurrences increase exponentially when the right skills and/ or talents are not utilized and the transfer of information and knowledge is not managed properly.

EFFECTIVE MANAGEMENT OF TECHNOLOGY

General Considerations

A key consideration in the effective management of technology is the dissemination of a large existing knowledge base for its usefulness to research and development projects. This information exists in the form of printed literature, microfiche; and, increasingly, digital tapes, optical discs, and other modern records. According to W.O. Baker:

> The volume of such information has now reached a level where it is frequently dealt with by ignoring it. Especially by-passed is action on increased data in many languages, and their storage in the recondite recesses of bibliography. It is easier to do it over than to look it up, some say.
>
> This doctrine overlooks the probability that you almost certainly will not get it right the first time over. More significantly, it omits the crucial and invaluable role of the organization of knowledge that does inhabit the literature, despite what a frustrated browser may think. Many a technical writer has used a career-long experience to put each item of discovery and interpretation into a wider context in the field. These efforts, properly covered, can aid the research and development program director to assess the promise and posture of fields being considered for commercial development.[13] *Reprinted with permission.*

It is the responsibility of research and development management to assure that a mechanism exists within the organization so that scientists and engineers can evaluate the literature before charging into expensive development programs.

The following recommendations are made for the management of technology:

- Make technology planning an integral part of business planning, recognizing the similarities and differences in these functions.
- Assure that applied research, technology, and its implementation, and business move in unison, staffing each area with the right skills and talents, encouraging and emphasizing communication and skill development.
- Assure that technology management has strong leadership to provide challenge, direction, and an open environment that allows room for individuality and flexibility yet keeps the overall direction towards meeting corporate business objectives.

The problem of developing an integrated plan is one of communication between business and technology, two specialties with widely different perspectives and characteristics. Technologists are characterized by the following attitudes and perspectives, which are enhanced by their educational process and the nature of science.

- Love of science for science sake
- Prefer to work in areas that interest them and challenge their imagination
- Greatest satisfaction comes from publication and peer recognition
- Enjoy dealing and communicating with other technologists rather than business people
- Limit planning to their area of interest and curiosity
- Like to get in-depth understanding of a problem irrespective of its practical utility
- Creative in an open environment rather than in one of restraint
- Introverted and private except with their colleagues

Business professionals, on the other hand, are characterized by the following attitudes and perspectives which are an outcome of their education and work environment:

- Lack of understanding in what it takes to accomplish technical objectives and risks involved in technical work

- Performance relies on fast input, despite the fact that technical processing of information takes time
- Tend to assign the same priority to all tasks, thus confusing technical counterparts about what is required and when
- Control oriented
- Consider short term results that have an impact on their business more important than strategic goals.

Such diverse characteristics tend to produce conflict between technology and business functions, a problem well recognized in academia and industry.[14,15] There are on-going concerns as how to improve the communication between these two very different groups. An excellent review article on changes in business and marketing education by Patricia W. Meyers and Parker Worthing[16] examines research about marketing education over the past 20 years and reveals some consistent abilities which practitioners deem necessary for well-prepared graduates.

"Taken together the reviewed articles reflect a growing concern and awareness that the nature of business and marketing management abilities is altering, particularly because of today's rapid changes in technologies, world markets, and communication capabilities. Some new or greatly revised abilities that seem to be evolving as important for marketers would include: 1) awareness of and an ability to communicate effectively with other functional areas in the organizations; 2) faster response times in all phases of the product life cycle; 3) innovativeness and creativity; 4) entrepreneurial skills; 5) longer term, strategic time frames for planning and decision making; and 6) industrial and competitive analysis." (p.245)[16] Based upon the foregoing review of recent articles, it appears that both academicians and practitioners are becoming increasingly aware that the nature of management, and with it that of marketing management, is changing.

Technology Portfolio

Since the strategic thinking process for both business and technology is similar, it can be used as a vehicle to bridge the gap between the two functions. An example is a technology portfolio, analogous to a business portfolio, which can be visualized as different aspects of technology required for maintaining and enhancing existing business — the cash generators — and applied research and technology developments for growth businesses. Between these two areas however, are a number of common technological attributes that can be used across a spectrum of businesses to enhance the competitive position.

These attributes are required for growth businesses but can also be effectively deployed for mature businesses without additional cost to the technology budget. The technology portfolio is shown in Figure 5.2.

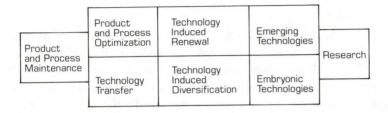

Figure 5.2   Technology Portfolio

The focus here is on internal as well as external technology developments relating to all aspects of business and covering a time horizon well into the future. Such an approach permits exploiting synergistic effects of technologies and skills, and provides a corporation a means to assure balance in its technology portfolio. It is a way to visualize the variety of skills needed over a wide range of technology capabilities and the way in which these skills can be exploited depending upon opportunities or threats.

The technology portfolio addresses the R&D need of a corporation. According to Roland W. Schmitt:

> No one will argue very much about the goal of R&D in a corporation: it is, quite simple, to lead and support innovation - product innovation and market innovation for new business development; materials innovation and process innovation for competitive advantage. This R&D occurs at all levels in a corporation and encompasses varying levels of risk and varying degrees of leverage. The most advanced R&D, usually at corporate level, must devote its energy overwhelmingly to highly leveraged opportunities - the ones that turn entire businesses around, or create entirely new businesses.... To produce such highly leveraged opportunities, one has to do forefront work on a balanced spectrum of programs.[17] *Reprinted with permission.*

Schmitt categorizes these programs as 1) today's focused and targeted projects; 2) work that will produce tomorrow's focused targeted projects; and 3) speculative or exploratory work. These categories form the heart of industrial research and development (R&D).

An ideal R&D organization is planned, managed and staffed to address the needs of the technology portfolio with a built in flexibility to support changing business needs. Thus, according to Schmitt

What one sees in a successful industrial laboratory are a lot of people who can work in all the various modes. . ., who can come through under pressure when working toward one of those focused targets; who can, when the occasion arises, perceive new targets for tomorrow; and who can, on yet other occasions, take off on an exploration of a new idea, or a campaign of research in a scientific frontier.[17] *Reprinted with permission.*

Such an organization is not created by throwing a large number of scientists and engineers together with loosely defined goals. A successful technology organization of which R&D is a major part is built recognizing technological needs of businesses. A major part of such an effort is training and developing skills and talents which, when put together, provide strong teams working towards common goals. The efficiency and effectiveness of a technology organization is a strong function of multiple skill development and technology leadership, which provides challenge, direction and environment for creative and innovative work.

Technology Planning

It must be recognized, however, that no amount of excellence in technology can be effective if it is mismatched with a company's business goals. Hence, a strong need to integrate technology and the business planning process exists at the corporate level.

Arthur D. Little, Inc. (ADL)[18] and Stacey and his colleagues at Battelle have done an excellent job in the area of formulating technology planning based on strategic business planning methodology. The ADL concepts were presented at the 1981 European Management Forum.

Strategic planning and strategy management techniques gained widespread acceptance in the 1970's but most of them failed to deal with the issue of how to deploy technology in support of corporate strategy. As a result, few companies integrate technology into their strategy formulation process and major technical choices are treated as a tactical rather than strategic decision or viewed largely as a concern of R&D.[18]

In the material presented at Davos, Switzerland, ADL, describes the strategic role of technology: "Technological innovations can be a source of great opportunity or major threat to a business. Technology must therefore be managed and deployed in support of both Business Unit and Corporate Strategies."

Technology can be deployed at three levels: corporate, sector, and strategic business unit. The three levels assure that short range (1 to

3 years), medium range (3 to 5 years) and long-range technological needs of the corporation are being addressed.

The concepts of experience curve and product life cycle have been used widely in planning technology despite the inherent risk in developing technology or business planning based on generic concepts. One aspect of technology, for example, process technology might be approaching maturity, yet the product technology which is based on customer needs might be changing radically and may provide new opportunities. To recognize and take advantage of these opportunities requires skills radically different from those being used in technology maintenance. The challenge for technology management is to recognize the changing business and technological needs and develop the mix of new skills to successfully exploit the business opportunities. Conventional organizations are too bureaucratic and loaded with inertia to recognize opportunities and to reorganize accordingly unless an intentional effort is made by top management.

Arthur D. Little — Approach to Technology Planning

Arthur D. Little's concepts of technology planning involve an integration of strategic, competitive, and technical information. The life cycle concept provides one part of this integration. Like industries, technologies are dynamic. They have life cycles and go through stages of maturity. The "maturity" concept was introduced by ADL in late 1960s as a useful way to describe the natural dynamics of industrial competition. It has been used successfully in this context since then and applied successfully to technology management since the late 1970s.

The development of technologies follow an S-shaped curve, rising from applied research, which is time consuming and costly, through development to implementation and full performance potential of the technology. Like industries, technology life cycle can be classified into four categories: embryonic or emerging, growth, mature, and aging. The time it takes for a technology to reach any one of these stages varies vastly from a few months to years; in some cases they never achieve their full potential and are abandoned in favor of more promising technologies. This concept is demonstrated in Figure 5.3.

The dotted lines indicate time spans of different technologies to reach the saturation limit. When that happens new technologies emerge providing better cost/performance than the previous technology and resulting in another S-shaped curve. Normally, development of new technology gets underway before an existing technology reaches its saturation limit.

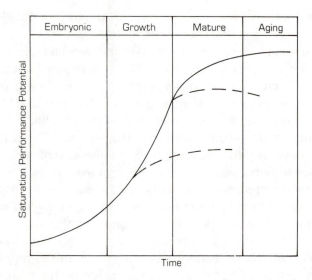

Figure 5.3 The S-shaped Curve of Technology Development[18]
Reprinted with permission.

An example of various technologies at different stages of the life cycle is shown in Figure 5.4.[19]

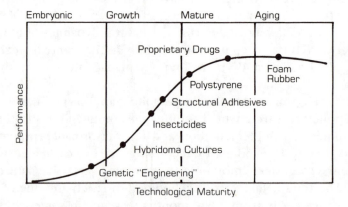

Figure 5.4 The Technology Maturity Cycle[19]
Reprinted with permission.

Embryonic technologies such as genetic engineering are usually recognized in early stages but their success in replacing mature technologies is uncertain. Such technologies are costly to develop but if successful they provide the highest profit potential. Growth technologies such as hybridoma cultures, insecticides, and structural adhesives which have gone through successful development provide a strong competitive position and are protected by process/product patents. Mature and aging technologies become standardized and provide little or no barrier to entry.

Independent of maturity, but critical to resource allocation decision-making, is the concept of competitive impact. This concept relates each technology to the product and the basis of competition in the industry. In other words, this concept supplies a link to business strategy and the perspective of market planner. The competitive impact of technology is defined as follows:

- *"Base* — those technologies necessary for participation in businesses, but having no competitive advantage.
- *"Key* — technologies critical to the basis of competition.
- *"Emerging/Pacing* — technologies in the development phase with a possibility of changing the basis of competition (becoming key technologies)." (p.33)[19]

This concept of technology investment vis-a-vis their future potential is shown in Figure 5.5.

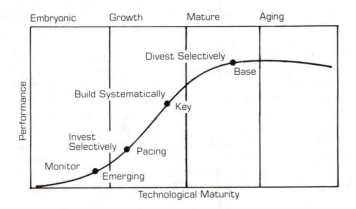

Figure 5.5   Technological Investment Mode[19]
Reprinted with permission.

Finally, technology competitive position, how a company stacks up to competitors, direct and indirect, is taken into account in the light of maturity and competitive impact to develop a portfolio approach to technology resource allocation decision consistent with business strategy and competitive and technological realities.

ADLs approach of integrating technological resources with the strategic planning process is based on the following principles:

- Every product is an outcome of a number of different technologies having different potentials for competitive impact.
- Technologies like products and industries go through different stages of life cycles.
- Competitors have different relative strengths in different technologies.
- Technology strategies should be an outcome of existing and anticipated technological and business opportunities and threats.

Battelle Approach to Technology Planning

Stacey of Battelle and his colleagues have taken a more fundamental approach in integrating technology and business strategy which can be summarized by the following conclusions: (1) R&D is only a part of the overall technology strategy; (2) the problem in integrating technology and business planning is the difficulty of communication between the business and technical staffs; (3) there is no integrating mechanism to help overcome these communication problems.[20]

One result is often an allocation of R&D budgets among business units based on less than optimum criteria, e.g., sales volume or current profitability rather than technological and business opportunities.

In response to the need to integrate business and technology planning, Stacey has developed an approach under the name of "B-TECH". This approach recognizes that technology planning is broader than just R&D planning, and that R&D planning, technology planning and business planning are interwoven. These interrelationships are shown in Figure 5.6 where the business strategy provides an envelope for technology strategy, which in turn has an R&D strategy as an important element.

B-TECH recognizes that business strategies involve more than technology, but that all technology strategies must fit within the total concept of the businesses where even basic R&D is not totally independent. In the same way a technology strategy is broader than just R&D and encompasses licensing, the purchase of technology, and other technology activities. All R&D strategy must fit the total corporate technology thrust. The B-TECH approach has 11 steps as shown in Figure 5.7. The approach starts with a business and technology segmentation of the firm. The next few steps separate the business and technology portions of the planning effort for several reasons:

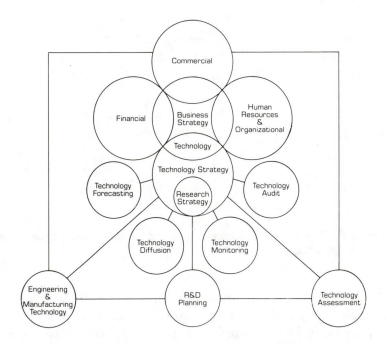

Figures 5.6   Interactions of Business and Technology Strategy[20]

Reprinted with permission.

- These two analyses require different inputs.
- Planning for the business and technology aspects of the firm is often in a different state of development within the company or the two have not been developed in a way that easily permits merging them.
- To create a corporate culture that promotes integration of technology and business and prevents one element from overwhelming the other. (Often the business aspects of planning submerge the technological ones in the customary analysis.)[20] *Reprinted with permission.*

After examining business and technology issues, the two elements are merged to show future effects on the firm's businesses. Alternative strategies are then postulated, a final strategy or set of strategies is selected, and resources are allocated based on this strategy. Implementation and control steps follow, during which variables defined by the various business and technology plans are monitored for change.

All in all, the *B-TECH* approach utilizes the strengths of portfolio planning concepts and integrates them with the strategic planning of technology.

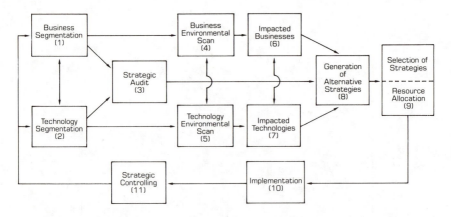

Figure 5.7 The B-TECH Approach to Integrating Technology and Business Strategy[20]
Reprinted with permission.

The concepts developed both by ADL and Battelle have a sound basis and their implementation requires a great deal of knowledge and judgment both in business and technology. The impact of technology's complexity is further compounded since it can be from raw materials, through processing, from customer's technologies or substitution threat by new products. Such a situation exists in each market segment and requires a focused effort to yield a meaningful evaluation. Unless these factors are recognized and built into the technology organization it is almost impossible to make use of technology planning concepts. The planning approaches developed by both ADL and Battelle take into consideration the complexities of planning and managing technology and their impact on businesses.

SUMMARY

The emergence and implementation of portfolio planning concepts during the 1970s resulted in aligning technology effort to various SBUs. In the 1980s it was recognized that segmentation of technology based on SBU concepts alone is not conducive to developing and deploying technology for competitive advantage because portfolio concepts do not address strategic planning and management of technology in the first place. The need for strategic planning of technology was recognized in the early 1980s and led to the development of technology planning techniques by a number of consulting companies which complement the portfolio planning concepts.

The development of these technology planning techniques by themselves is of no use unless corporations realize their importance and make a strong effort to implement them in concert with business planning to gain competitive edge and/or enhance a business position. Such planning points out areas of threat and opportunity, the need for development of skills and talents well head of time and provides a rational way of resource allocation. Technology planning should never be introduced for budget reduction; in fact, should this occur, the total technology planning effort will have been wasted and result in a setback to the institution of technology planning in the future.

As has been the case in strategic business planning and implementation, strategic planning of technology is a long, challenging and laborious process requiring the commitment of top management and an educational program to explain its usefulness both to technologists and business professionals. When successfully implemented, its rewards will be a strong business/technology competitive thrust and an assurance that the business enterprise will be a viable entity for future decades.

REFERENCES

1. Schulman, R., Clark, E.: R&D score board. *Business Week*, July 8, 1985, pp. 86-106.

2. Arnoldo, H.C., Mafluf, N.S.: The use of the industry attractiveness business strength matrix. *Interfaces* 13: 54-71, 1983.

3. Kantrow, A.M.: Keeping informed. *Harvard Business Review*, 58: 6-18, 1980.

4. Abell, D.F., Hammond, J.: Strategic Market Planning. Englewood Cliffs, Prentice Hall, NJ, 1979.

5. Hayes, R.H., Abernathy, W.J.: Managing our way to economic decline. *Harvard Business Review* 1980, 58: 67-77

6. Porter, M.E.: Competitive Strategy. The Free Press, NY, 1980.

7. Ehrlich, E.: America expects too much from its entrepreneurial heroes. *Business Week*. July 28, 1986, p. 33.

8. Encyclopedia Britannica, Vol. 18, ed 15. William Benton, Helen Hemingway: Publisher, Chicago, pp. 1973, 50-54.

9. Allen, T.J.: *Managing the Flow of Technology*. MIT Press, Cambridge, 1977.

10. Jones, H., Twiss, C.B.: *Forecasting Technology for Planning Decisions.* PBI, New York, 1978.

11. Krulee, G.K., and Nadler, E.B.: Studies of education for science and engineering: Student values and curriculum choice. IEEE Transactions on Engineering Management, 1960, 7: 146-158.

12. Facts and Figures for Chemical R&D, Chemical Engineering News, July 22, 1985, pp. 28-43.

13. Baker, W.O.: R&D Complexity and Competition. Research and Development Key Issues for Management. Conference Board Report No. 842, 1983, p. 4.

14. Laric, M.V., Tucker, L.R.: Toward greater accountability in higher education: The case for a responsive marketing curricula in Connecticut. *New England Journal of Business Economics* 6: 15-31, 1979.

15. Murphy, P.E., Laczniak, E.R.: Marketing Education: Current Status and a View for 1980's. Monograph series #11, American Marketing Association, Chicago, 1980.

16. Meyers, P.W., Worthing, P.M.: Marketing Educators As Artists: Lessons From History and Beyond, Southern Marketing Association Proceedings, November 1984, pp. 243-246.

17. Schmitt, W.R.: When Pendulum Swings Toward Applied Research. Research and Development Key Issues for Management. Conference Board, Report No. 842, 1983, pp. 13-15.

18. Arthur D. Little: *Strategic Management of Technology, European Management Forum, Davos,* 1981.

19. Arthur D. Little: Maturing Chemical Businesses - An Approach to Renewal. October 1983/R831001.

20. Stacey, G.S.: B-TECH, An Approach for Integrating Technology and Business Strategy, Battelle Memorial Institute, Columbus, Ohio.

ROLE OF TOP MANAGEMENT IN THE EFFECTIVE UTILIZATION OF TECHNOLOGY

1 2 3 4 5 6 7 8 9 10

TOP MANAGEMENT'S PERCEPTION OF TECHNOLOGY

The perception of research and development (R&D) by top management is well described by J.E. Goldman, retired Senior Vice President and Chief Scientist of Xerox Corporation.

R&D is a "black box" to top management. The computer analogy may be a very appropriate one. Like computers, the black box of R&D has input ports, output ports, and perhaps a few feedback loops and peripherals tied into it. Constituted as it is by lawyers, salesmen and bean counters, top management is usually not conversant with the inner workings of the black box. It looks to the output . . . the impact on the product line, or the process that make the product. It has a notion that there is probably a linear relationship between the output and input (the personnel and resources that are committed by the enterprise). Since these resources are a drain on the earnings, top management would love to see an amplification factor introduced so that that input is minimized while output is optimized. Thus, it expects that R&D will enhance the profitability of the corporate enterprise. There are inherent risks in each of the elements of the R&D black box.[1] *Reprinted with permission.*

These risks can be minimized by emphasizing the importance of excellence and above average professionals in the R&D organization. It is the quality and not quantity alone of these professionals which results in successful R&D. The purpose of R&D is both defensive and offensive. It allows the corporation to gain a competitive advantage through the improvement of existing products and processes, and the development of innovative new products.

Top management must assure that R&D management is of proven high calibre, since it is the R&D management that understands the working of the "black box" and what needs to be done for optimum results. A successful R&D organization will produce papers that are published, it will provide new products, and it will improve processes and existing products.[1]

The above criteria alone, although necessary, are not sufficient for successful R&D. In today's changing business environment, an integrated technology/business plan and its implementation is a key requirement for maintaining a strong competitive position.

TOP MANAGEMENT'S RESPONSIBILITY FOR TECHNOLOGY

In both technology and business planning, the active participation of top management is essential.[2,3] Technology and business managements must understand each other's needs and constraints. This is the first step in bridging the gap between the two. The effort also requires participation of middle management and professionals from both areas. In fact, it is almost impossible to prepare a business/technology plan unless the organization as a whole participates. The degree, level, and type of participation varies vastly from top management to professionals. The participation of top functional management is critical in the planning process and it should be led by a manager responsible for the business unit.

The existing concepts of strategic business planning, irrespective of the approach employed, are strongly based upon perceived markets, growth, and ROI. Resources are deployed depending upon the resulting classification of each business. Technology resources are similarly allocated based on the position of businesses in the corporate portfolio.

Such an allocation can result in growth businesses being weighted down by a heavy technology budget, because of their need for diverse skills to exploit technology opportunities under a time pressure created by markets and competitive forces. These businesses are often incapable of utilizing those resources to the fullest. The mature businesses could utilize the excess resources, particularly of support functions, to maintain and enhance their competitive position. However, they are incapable of doing so because of their position in the business evaluation grid. The result is a paradox in which corporations are willing to pay for inefficient use of human resources in technology rather than use those resources for enhancing the business position of mature and marginal businesses. Poor utilization of human resources, apart from waste, also impacts the present and future caliber of these resources which tend to become stagnant, demoralized, and obsolete when they are not challenged to the fullest. Technology management is afraid to bring these issues to top management's attention, since this will create a tendency to force personnel reductions and again raises the major issue of which talents and skills can be reduced. The reduction issue is complex since some talents and skills are used to the fullest while others, although needed, have only partial utilization. The result is reflected in an imbalance of technology budgets which ultimately has adverse impacts on all businesses whether mature, growth, embryonic, or declining.

Technology Planning

To correct this situation, technology planning must be undertaken with corporate strategic business planning. This concept is reflected in a simplified business/technology plan model designed to bring technology and business concerns together at the same level with equal emphasis and start thinking of technology as an integral part of business planning (Fig. 6.1).

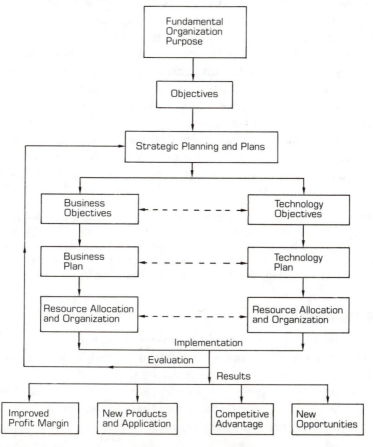

Figure 6.1   Integrated Technology/Business Plan Model

The fundamental organization purpose reflects the type of businesses in which top management would like to be. This is based on their evaluation of strengths and weaknesses of the organization and the strategic fit of various businesses, and leads to outlining the overall organization objectives for both financial and nonfinancial criteria. Together, these set up a tone for the strategic planning process, which in this model, addresses both business and technology issues as equally important in the business evaluation of product lines, new products, and acquisitions. An important part of such a consideration is to assure the exploitation of synergistic effects of different technologies and to place an emphasis on effective utilization of technology while taking into account skills, talents, and communications. These are key factors to be addressed as the planning process moves to functional and organizational levels, which in turn generate short and long term budgets. The planning process also addresses implementation and evaluation, which is fed back to the original plan and reiterated until most of the organization is in concert with the plans. It is not wise to use quick fix strategies for integrating business and technology since this would dilute the thinking process essential to the whole idea of the planning exercise. Plans prepared from the models with little thought to originality end up as a paper exercise, generating large amounts of reports and producing minimal results. The planning process should be action oriented and must show results within a foreseeable time horizon.

The same conclusion was reached by a working group of the European Industrial Research Management Association (EIRMA), headquartered in Paris. Their findings were published in Research Management, May-June 1985:

> If there is no formal R&D (technology) input to strategic planning in a company, then it is hard to see how that company can rationally determine what or how much R&D is needed . . . R&D management should not just wait for questions to be asked by others; it is expected to be aggressive on behalf of R&D and to take initiative.[4]

Technology Charter

The effective utilization of technology depends upon 1) an integrated planning of technology and business; and 2) management of technology to assure optimum resource utilization.

In a corporation, technology is deployed at a number of different levels. The overall emphasis for technology development and deployment and its importance to the businesses must come from top management. Providing funds alone, although important, is inadequate without setting an overall direction.

A key issue then is the nature of the charter of technology within the corporation. One can argue that the charter is different for different groups and divisions. Its importance to the businesses, however, should be reflected and conveyed by top management. The charter should reflect top management values and expectations of technology and complement the corporations aspirations and objectives. Examples might be to:

- Support the achievement of business objectives through technical excellence
- Offer cost effective products and services ahead of or better than competition

These broad statements set a tone for an integration of technology with business. It leads to further thought on how this should be accomplished within a corporation with multiple businesses of a diverse nature.

Many of the corporations are now being managed in a decentralized/differential mode. This type of management delegates total business and other functional responsibilities to groups and divisions that carry out their operation within corporate guidelines. This is accomplished through the development, acceptance and, execution of a strategic plan which mainly addresses financial and market issues. Progress is followed through quarterly returns vs. projections. Little attention is paid to technology, except as it influences manufacturing or achievement of short-term market objectives. Corporations presently have no means of checking technology effort on an on-going basis, since by nature technical work has a much longer time horizon before results are evident. By the time the business feels the adverse impact of mismanaged technology, it is too late for correction through a redirection of technical effort. The ultimate result is a loss of competitive position and opportunities.

Another area of importance is to assure that the technology effort is not sacrificed by business to meet short-term objectives. Decentralized businesses, where management authority has been delegated to the SBU level, are particularly vulnerable here. Failure to hold appropriate technology spending levels virtually guarantees that today's cash generators will become tomorrow's declining businesses.

Especially in growth businesses where technology plays a prominent role, the benefits of integrating business and technology are particularly important. These areas tend to over-hire with the misconception that more scientists and engineers, and consequently higher budgets, will produce faster technical results and enhance the business position. However, it is neither the number of scientists nor the dollar amount of a budget alone that produces the best results. Rather, it is the quality of technology leadership in combination with planning, the right mix of skills and talents, and the work environment that results in a focused technology effort and leads to business success.

In corporations where authority and responsibility are delegated to the operating group, corporate management must ensure that long range concerns are being adequately supported and that the personnel assigned to such programs have the requisite skills.

Overall, the 3M concept that "products are the business divisions' responsibility, but, technologies belong to 3M and their synergistic effect should be exploited throughout the corporation"[5] makes sense for small or large corporations.

The technology charter of sub-units within the corporation must support the corporate charter. Groups and divisions must include technology input for business evaluation of each product line ranging from raw materials through finished products to end use markets. Particular attention must be focused on impacts of technology on suppliers and using industries. A simple question, "What can technology do for a product line, in its entirety?" is the first step in initiating a technology plan. This question leads to information gathering, process and market evaluation, and competitive analysis. The end result is a definition of opportunities and threats to the product line. Based on this analysis, one can categorize needs on a tactical/short-term, and strategic/long-term basis. A combination of technical and business input is necessary to develop a combined strategy for each product line which leads to optimal resource allocation and program follow through. The overall resource allocation will depend upon top management commitment to each business, which depends upon business' profit and growth potential.

TECHNOLOGY MANAGEMENT

Significance

In 1985, total R&D funding in the United States was estimated to be $106.6 billion, which included $49.8 billion by the federal government, $53.2 billion by industry, $2.3 billion by universities and colleges, and $1.3 billion by non-profit organizations.[6] About 70 percent of the federal funding is for defense, which has doubled since 1981; and over half of the total federal R&D funding is contracted through industry. Thus, industry spent about $78 billion dollars for R&D funding in 1985. When funds of this magnitude are being spent, we must think deeply about managing it for the interest of the firm, the public, and the nation. On the average, diversified corporations spend 40 to 70 percent of pretax income on R&D.

"Is this investment for the future being suitably evaluated and managed to assure ability in international competition?" (p.2)[7]

The magnitude of R&D management's responsibilities and complexities are described by W.O. Baker.[7]

> They reach into strategic arenas; they link the public and private purposes, and they must pursue goals on a scale previously considered to be too large for scientists and engineers. And this is happening at a time when the actual content of science and engineering is of unprecedented complexity, and is being subjected to global competition. These responsibilities extend into bold and drastic revisions of cooperation and coordination of international trade, competitive machinery such as patenting and proprietorship of software, publications and regulatory processes. There remains as well the obvious and familiar ones of tax mechanisms, credit programs, and, above all, human resources and education. Obviously the kind of competition now pressing on all of U.S. industry, and the complication of industrial R&D requiring ever-closer links with these general management issues, call for improved organizing and managing.[7] *Reprinted with permission.*

Further, Baker cites some of the salient features which point to the demanding task of integrating R&D management with issues relating to public policy, market economics, corporate culture, and the specific financial and working conditions of particular enterprises.

- It now takes about nine years after discovery of a new drug for it to be approved for use in the United States
- The increased U.S. dependence on foreign products is resulting in high trade deficits. In 1960, U.S. dependence on international trade was less than 10 percent of GNP, in 1982 it was 25 percent of GNP and it is increasing.
- France, Japan, and West Germany each devotes 10 to 15 percent of government supported R&D to industrial application. The United States devotes less than 1 percent for this purpose
- United States space and defense (R&D) spending is about $36 billion, 50 percent more than that of Japan, West Germany and France put together.

- United States intrinsic industrial spending for R&D is of about the same magnitude as the total spent for industry by both government and privately in Japan, France, and West Germany. (p.3)[7]

The above loosely knit factors point toward a focused approach in the management of R&D function to provide a comprehensive edge in international markets.

Allocating Technology Resources

Technology funding should be based on the following criteria:

- The role of technology in a corporation's growth and business development
- Its independence from economic cycles, and concurrent within the realities of the business environment
- Its consideration as a risk, insurance for the future, and a strategic opportunity
- Its approval from a level which comprehends both the marketplace and technology realities implicit in the points above. There is a danger when technologists alone conceive and execute technology projects.

Technical resource deployment should consider the following:

- How much resources are to be deployed for tactical, short-term, and long-term needs, i.e., profit maintenance, enhancement, and future growth
- How well technology can stay in concert with overall businesses over time
- What impact changes in business direction might have on technology funding and management
- How well the synergism between different functional groups will be exploited
- How creative and innovative the technology is based on assessment of technology portfolio

Technology funds are allocated to meet a number of requirements, which can be divided into six categories:

- Maintenance and enhancement of existing businesses and technologies
- Non-economic technical objectives such as environmental and process safety
- Technical economic objectives which relate to cost reduction and process improvements

- Development of new products identified in the strategic business plan
- New business development either by acquisition of businesses or technologies
- Funding for support functions

The effective utilization of technology funds requires careful planning, managing, and evaluation. The projects must be staffed depending upon the skills and talents required to accomplish the best results, rather than make do with whatever happens to be available in the sponsoring department. To achieve this requires an interdisciplinary transfer of professionals and management flexibility, a difficult thing to accomplish since each unit tends to hoard its resources. An organizational philosophy of flexibility and cooperation is to everybody's advantage, because a mutually reciprocal arrangement is more likely to enhance the chances of success and earn top management respect for technology and technologists. The other essential part of technology management is to provide strong technical leadership to assure the direction of work. In such an organization innovation and creativity are almost the outcome of day-to-day operation. On the other hand, any emphasis on innovation or creativity in the absence of these criteria is an exercise in futility.

Technology Inefficiencies

A large number of technology organizations suffer from the inefficiencies shown in Figure 6.2, which result from not integrating business and technology and lack of top management attention. These inefficiencies result from: 1) inadequate planning and communication between business and technology; and 2) project failure and inefficient use of resources. The latter is caused by: 1) the wrong mix of skills; 2) a lack of direction; 3) a lack of technical leadership; 4) a lack of creativity and innovation; and 5) a lack of flexibility. These factors are further enhanced by interdepartmental politics.

If technology and business are properly integrated and an open environment of work is established, one can largely ameliorate the problems causing major inefficiencies in technology.

Figure 6.3 shows the impact of three major factors in the effective management of technology:

1. Integrating technology and business
2. Providing challenge, direction and utilizing synergistic effects of different technologies
3. Providing strong technology leadership, multiple skills development, and an open environment

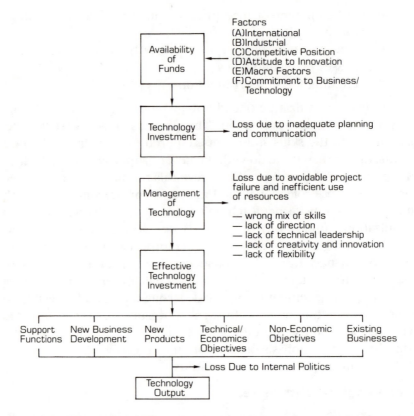

Figure 6.2   Flow of Funds for a Technology Organization

Curve *A* reflects an organization where these three factors are not taken into consideration, and top management believes that providing funds based on strategic business methodology alone is the key to technology success. Curves *B, C* and *D* show the incremental effects of recognizing the importance of the three factors in the management of technology. The overall impact in moving from Curve *A* to *D* is a dramatic improvement in technology productivity. The enhancement in technology productivity is due to the value added component of each action as indicated on the respective curves.

Technology Effectiveness

Chemical Week interviewed eight top technology managers to determine what factors are taken into consideration to determine research productivity.[8] The companies were: Exxon, Dupont, Rohm and Haas, Monsanto, Shell Development, Air Products and Chemicals, Johnson and Johnson, and one anonymous director of a medium sized company.

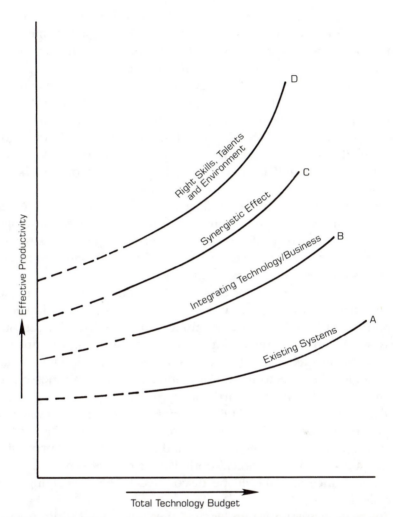

Figure 6.3 Incremental Impacts on Technology Productivity

Based on the results of these interviews the overall criteria for R&D productivity can be classified into two categories — qualitative and quantitative.

Most of the companies rely more on qualitative measures, such as success of technology in the market place, top management image of R&D and comparison of R&D costs with competitors. Exxon and Dupont, on the other hand, rely more on quantitative criteria such as profits generated by research programs in previous years and number of patents and publications.

The elusive nature of determining R&D effectiveness is well described by Robert A. Fuller, corporate vice president of Johnson & Johnson. Fuller has found that there are basically two ways to appraise research, "its either good or bad;"[8] however, he has found one qualitative method that tells whether research is "worth its money or not."[8] Querying enough people in manufacturing and marketing Fuller says, will tell "if technical service has been of help."[8]

Brian M. Rushton, Vice President Research and Development, Air Products, points out that measuring research productivity is definitely difficult. "There are so many intangibles that can't be measured, and they are often more important than numbers."[8] Fuller goes much further by saying that, if a research director has to go as far as using "equations and formulas to evaluate his department, he's in trouble."[8]

Unlike business, technology effectiveness is impossible to measure on a short-term basis. Its evaluation criteria have to be developed specific to the nature of business and technology. Any assessment must classify technology efforts in one of the following categories: tactical/short term or strategic/long term.

Each one of these categories should be evaluated based on the following criteria: 1) probability of success versus capital and expense exposure; 2) impacts of overspending and time delay on the businesses; 3) impact of technology failure on business; 4) impact of changes in market place on technology resources; 5) tangible and non-tangible benefits to the corporation and various businesses; and 6) measurable means of future improvements.

The above factors should be the premises of technology evaluation and must be comprehensible by top management. The criteria should have the concurrence of the middle managers and professionals responsible. Also technical optimism or enthusiasm, essential to success as they are, should be discounted when developing these premises.

Top management must understand the above implications to avoid short-term business fluctuations from becoming a major disruption in technology development. Market uncertainties and their impact on technology development should be continuously monitored. This is an important part in developing effectiveness criteria and should be spelled out clearly.

SUMMARY

The technology fit to the corporate strategy must be evaluated in its entirety. As business strategies change with environment, time, and other macro and micro factors, their impact on technology resources must be assessed. It should be determined what kind of technology flexibility exists and if the corporation should reconsider the whole technology strategy to build in more flexibility. A major part of such assessment is the commitment to the businesses. In-house vs. outside development of technology is a part of such considerations. There are also certain common functions which service or support all the technology areas. These functions are critical to the success of the whole technology effort and must be viewed as ingredients rather than as an auxiliary to technology, and explicitly included, evaluated, and judged as part of the technology plan.

The discussions in this chapter are well summarized in a *Business Week* article dated July 8, 1985, which gives a detailed breakdown of R&D spending based on industry structure and refers to the fact that even the best research is of little use unless it is moved out of the laboratory and into the market place. "The Japanese have obviously been much, much better than us when it comes to taking new technology and doing something with it,"[9] says Jules J. Duga of Battelle Memorial Institute. To reach such a level, first top management must recognize the value of technology and its impact on businesses and pay attention to its planning and management.

Further, management must recognize that it is neither the number of scientists nor the dollar amount alone that produces the best results. It is the quality of technology leadership in combination with planning, the right mix of skills and talents, and the work environment that results in a focused technology effort that leads to business success.

Technologists must be viewed, evaluated, and judged as the largest entity of cumulative brainpower within the corporation. The outcome of technology must reflect and fulfill those expectations by its forceful and positive impact on businesses.

REFERENCES

1. Goldman, J.E.: R&D: The Major Risks, Research and Development Key Issues for Management; The Conference Board, Report No. 842, 1983, p. 7.

2. Neuschel, R.F.: The Chief Executive's Strategic Role and Responsibilities. AMA, Special Study No. 5; 1977.

3. Steiner, G.A.: *Top Management Planning.* Macmillan, Inc., NY, 1969.

4. How Much R&D? *Research Management* 28: 28-29, 1985.

5. Krugh, L.C.: Seminar on Corporate Development, New York, March 5, 1985.

6. Facts and figures for chemical R&D. *Chemical Engineering News,* July 22, 1985, p. 30.

7. Baker, W.O.: R&D Complexity and Competition. Research and Development: Key Issues for Management; The Conference Board; Report No. 842, 1983, pp. 2-3.

8. Spalding, B.J.: How Research Managers Weigh Productivity, *Chemical Week,* January 1-8, 1986, 47-49.

9. Schulman, R., Clarke, E.: R&D Score Board. *Business Week,* July 8, 1985, p. 87.

ROLE OF TECHNOLOGY IN NEW BUSINESS DEVELOPMENT

1234567890

NEW BUSINESS DEVELOPMENT

The purpose of new business development is to gain competitive advantage and enhance the profit potential of a corporation. This can occur through either internal development, acquisitions, or both.

In the Conference Board Report No. 876 on competitive leverage, a number of authors expressed their opinions on how to gain competitive advantage. William D. Smithburg[1] emphasizes four basic steps for gaining a competitive edge: better market research to identify customers' future needs and capitalize on these future needs; the development of innovative products to satisfy those needs; an aggressive marketing policy to get the products across to the customers; financially successful total effort of research, development and marketing. In the same article Smithburg cites and wonders about the high failure rate of new products despite the use of sophisticated market research tools. He assesses one of the major reasons for failure:

> As a new product moves through the three step process of market research, product development, and strategy formulation, it often picks up a momentum of its own from bright, young, middle-management "advocates", who take up the banner at each step. They put their ego completely on the line behind the effort at each step. The resulting momentum makes it harder for them or for anyone to consider stopping a product with major negative features, but marketers have to do so.[1]

In addition to the four points mentioned by Smithburg, a large number of new products fail because they do not integrate technology and business. It is the technologist's job to develop a cost effective product identified by the market research that meets certain performance characteristics. If the product development effort is not in concert with marketing or vice versa, one or more of several adverse things can happen; high production costs, subminimal product performance or product quality, or major environmental and other regulatory concerns.

New business development can take one or more of the following forms: 1) new product development; 2) acquisitions/mergers or joint ventures; 3) development of new uses for existing products; 4) development and implementation of cost-effective technology for existing products but new to the company; 5) major cost reduction of existing products resulting in larger market share; 6) expansion of existing product lines into new geographical areas; 7) improved performance of existing products; and 8) development of second or third generation products.

Most successful corporations employ all of these methods for new business development. The type of strategy employed can vary vastly, depending upon which of the above routes is selected, yet the basic emphasis is the same, satisfying a customer's needs through market and technology development and implementation. The overall thrust is to increase the profit potential of the corporation.

Existing Status

In the existing system of managing diversified corporations — where businesses are divided into strategic business units, groups, sectors, and corporate arenas — the thrust towards new business development is carried out at all levels. For instance, acquisitions and mergers of a magnitude that impact the corporation as a whole are handled at the corporate level, eg, the RCA merger with GE or Searle's acquisition by Monsanto. However, the acquisition, which enhances only a product line's position, be it vertical integration or horizontal diversification of a synergistic business or technology, is handled at the strategic business unit or group level. The acquisitions that impact a number of strategic business units will be handled at sector level.

Similarly, the new product development efforts are carried out at the SBU, sector, and corporate levels. The SBUs new product development effort is directed toward development of second or third generation products or technologies, development of new uses for existing products, and expansion of existing product lines into new geographical areas. This effort normally has a time horizon of one to three years. The sector's development effort is focused on exploiting synergistic effects of a number of technologies and markets which cut across various businesses and have a time horizon of three to five years. At the corporate level the emphasis is toward the development of novel products and technologies which can generate new businesses over a time horizon of ten years or more.

In highly decentralized corporations like Johnson & Johnson, each business unit is managed as a separate company, and all the new business development tasks must be carried out by the SBU. By contrast, 3M manages its new business development at three different levels: SBU, sector, and corporate level.

Irrespective of where the new business development effort is handled, its success is highly dependent upon a knowledge of customers' needs, the markets and the competition. Also, the company must have technological strengths capable of developing and deploying new products to fulfill the needs and make the total effort a profitable venture to the corporation. Any new business development involves a number of risks, be they technological or market oriented. The magnitude of these risks can be minimized by having a business plan which considers both market and technological issues and by evaluating the effort at different stages of business development.

The two major components of a business are *products/markets* and *technology*. The management of these functions is highly dependent upon the nature of the business. The key questions of centralization vs. decentralization and which mode is useful are a strong function of the nature of the business and the extent of management competence. For example, in emerging businesses a decentralized effort with a high degree of mobility is a must, but in mature businesses, where the technologies and products/markets have a high degree of synergism, a centralized management mode may be preferable. The key selection criteria should be based on strategic thrusts rather than tactical concerns — in short, no business unit should be allowed to stagnate except those clearly classified for divestiture. Most mature businesses are in need of technological and/or market rejuvenation. However, the myopic view where both the technology and business functions are too ingrained in their routines and unable to visualize innovative ideas for product or process rejuvenation is a common problem. To counteract this, management must allow the same spirit of risk taking in mature businesses as in new business areas. The magnitude of the risk, however, varies vastly depending upon the opportunity or threat.

Today, industry faces a problem that is an outcome of events in the 1970s that resulted in certain attitudes which have been ingrained in management. This has been well described by John Welch, CEO of General Electric, in his address to the Conference Board's 1981 Marketing Conference.

> So in using the word "marketing", I mean the attitude...not the function ... the primacy of marketing as a total company perspective... My shorthand for the meaning of marketing as a management concept would be: *constant innovation in a world of constant change*...
>
> The seventies, with all those cost-shocks - energy costs, inflation costs, capital costs - were hardly conducive to real strategy... real innovation ... the long view. We sought "sure things" - who wouldn't in turbulent times? But sure things go against the grain of the idea of marketing, which, as I said - reflecting change and life itself - insists on constant innovation.
>
> The desire for sure things, and the long- view vacuum left by marketing brought on strategic planning. At financial planning, at resource allocation - the internalities ... strategic planning did well ... but not too well at marketing ... the crucial externality. Comfortable with quantification, strategic planning *managed* the external world beautifully - market size and share, it made huge contributions to resource allocation ... but strategic planning didn't, or couldn't *chart a course*.... It didn't navigate ... it didn't lead ... and unfortunately, too often it was seen to replace marketing.[2] *Reprinted with permission.*

If a corporation can staff, organize, and manage successful efforts of new product development, results will be a continuous stream of new business opportunities, some more successful than others. The key, however, is planning for such an effort by considering all aspects before allocating large resources in anticipation of fast results. This effort must be built in stages, with the assurance that each stage complements and enhances the next stage. *More often than not, new product development becomes synonymous with the magnitude of the budget rather than a planned approach of identifying, evaluating, selecting, and staffing the projects with the right skills/ talents.*

New Product Development

Planning

Planning for new product development challenges a corporation's technology and business functions to the utmost. A strong team with skills in business and technology, plus a strong plan to integrate the two is absolutely necessary for success. To get these diverse functions working with each other, new product development areas must have strong support, guidance, and commitment from top corporate management.

The basic reason for the development of new products is to maintain or enhance business position. The environment in which a corporation operates consists of customers; competitors; and suppliers; plus economic, political and social factors. As the environment changes, it creates both opportunities and threats for existing businesses. New products and services are developed to satisfy these changing needs, be it consumer related or industrial products. New product development can take several forms, such as the extension or modification of existing products, development of entirely new products, or production and sales of existing products which are new to the corporation.

Invariably, the successful new products are an outcome of both "market pull" and "technology push". No one corporation can participate in all the markets; hence, it is important to know what the corporate strategy is before venturing into areas of new product development. Each corporation has its ultimate objectives, its competence, and its constraints, which govern the markets in which they want to participate. The responsibility of new product development varies depending upon whether it is oriented to consumer or industrial goods. In consumer-oriented businesses, marketing plays a leadership role in the development of new products; whereas in industrial goods, business, marketing, and technology should jointly carry out new product development. In actual practice, however, the widely observed differences between marketing's and technology's objectives, time constraints, and mode of thinking causes technology to play a passive role and leaves the lead effort to marketing. This is one of the major reasons for the failure of new products in the industrial sector.

New product development is highly dependent upon the nature of the industry and technology in which a business is participating. For example, the Environmental Protection Agency requires that agricultural chemical companies establish a series of strict procedures for testing new products and documenting their results. These strict demands are reflected by costly in-house testing procedures. In this type of industry the product life cycle is long, but so is the development time.

High tech industries are primarily driven by new product development, since technological improvements can be made relatively easily. In these industries product life cycle is short and product obsolescence is a major threat. To stay or even survive in these businesses, new product development and their introduction to the marketplace is a must.

Businesses which deal with industrial goods have relatively stable markets, and new product development is mostly an extension of existing products. Technological changes, although significant, tend to be incremental. In these businesses, continued success is a strong function of production costs and maintaining a proactive stance towards customer's needs. Customer's needs are frequently affected by changing technology and the introduction of substitution products. While the potential of substitution constitutes a threat to the existing products, it also provides an opportunity for new product development.

Irrespective of what business a corporation is involved with, new product development requires a certain sequence of tasks. Some of these must be done sequentially, while others can be done simultaneously. The different stages of new product development are shown in Figure 7.1.

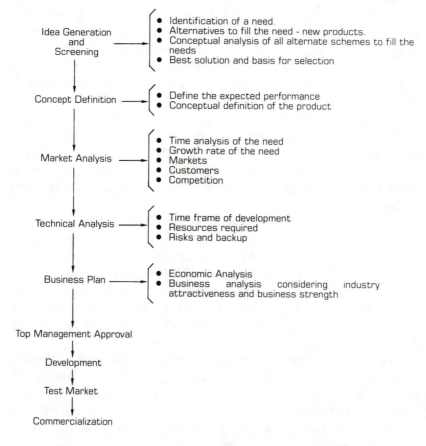

Figure 7.1   Stages of New Product Development

The new product development effort involves a number of different functions in the planning process and requires a considerable amount of time and effort in the initial phase. Thus, it is imperative that some criteria be assigned by which one product is selected over another. For example, the criterion followed by 3M is shown in Figure 7.2. 3M assesses ideas for new product development on the basis of business strength and novelty of the products.[3] If a product is new to the world and 3M *has* no business strength, it would consider acquiring market expertise; if a product is new to the world and 3M *has* business strength, it is considered to be most promising. When a product is not new to the world, ie, it could be a "me too" product or an extension of existing products, either the inventor is encouraged to take his idea outside or it is taken over by the existing business units, if business strength exists. The acceptance of an idea leads to a business plan. This plan is frequently reassessed during the course of the program to determine funding continuation or program cancellation.

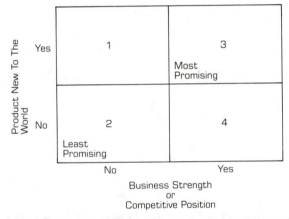

Quadrant 1 - If successful consider acquiring marketing expertise
Quadrant 2 - Inventor encouraged to go outside 3M
Quadrant 3 - Most promising
Quadrant 4 - Should fit one of the existing divisions

Figure 7.2   New Product Evaluation Criteria

Identification of Need or Idea Generation

The key to new product development is identification of a need, which is an outcome of idea generation. Creativity is considered to be a prerequisite to idea generation and is defined as the generation of usable new ideas. By and large most people are creative, but the degree of creativity varies. Why some people are more creative than others has been the subject of numerous studies.[4] It is a well known fact that children, particularly between the ages of three to eight, are more creative than adults.[5] As children grow into adulthood, the level of awareness increases but creativity does not increase proportionally. In fact, it has been proven that creativity and intelligence have no correlation. A higher education does not promote creativity, but increases the level of knowledge in the fields of specialization. A higher knowledge base by itself provides little utility to society unless it can be used for socio-economic purposes. Most educated people contribute to the socio-economic end, but the value added varies vastly and is not directly related to their level of education. A creative person can visualize a number of related and unrelated events and come up with usable new ideas. This process is well described by Twiss[6] (Fig. 7.3).

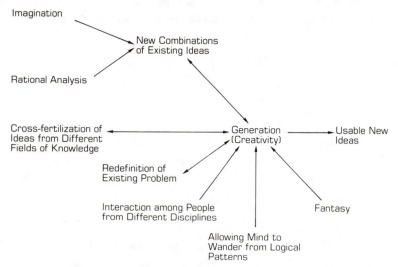

Figure 7.3   Process Leading to New Ideas[6]
Reprinted with permission.

The double headed arrows indicate the synergistic effects of the process, which leads to generation of even more ideas. Figure 7.3 illustrates that the generation of new ideas is a combination of a number of interactions utilizing multiple disciplines, inputs from people of various backgrounds, redefinitions of the problems, and of course a free thinking, nonbiased and unconventional way of looking at the environment.

Since idea generation is the first step in new product development, how do the organizations handle it? Ideally, new product ideas should come from people located throughout the organization; in real life, however, this is not true. Most people become so involved with their assignments that routine takes over for creativity. Top management needs to recognize that asking people to generate new ideas is likely to accomplish very little and that a concentrated effort has to be made. This effort can take one of several forms from venture teams to the creation of a new function within the corporation. A number of qualitative techniques have been developed to foster creativity and can be classified into two categories.

1. Creativity-spurring techniques which aim to free the mind from subconscious constraints; for example, brainstorming, synectics, lateral thinking.
2. Systematic analysis to reveal gaps which might be filled by future developments; for example, morphology, gap analysis, monitoring.

The use of these techniques alone is not likely to be successful unless an organization has made a strong commitment to the area of new product development. The organization must provide the overall environment to support these techniques, motivate all employees as to the importance of this function, and set up a systematic way of conducting them. The characteristics of such an organization are shown in Figure 7.4.

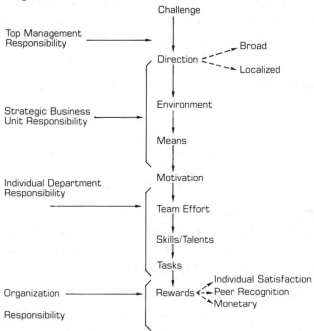

Figure 7.4   Characteristics of an Organization with Commitment to Innovation

It is top management's responsibility to provide realistic challenges to the strategic units, sectors or arenas. These challenges should include new product development in broad business areas that the corporation aspires to be in and should consider the competence level within the corporation. The challenge must include both strategic and tactical components. The strategic component addresses the new process and product development area and should be the responsibility of each SBU, irrespective of its position in the portfolio grid. Businesses marked for divestitures are an exception. It becomes the responsibility of each sector and SBU to provide the challenge, direction, environment, and means for a creative organization. Such a mode of operation should result in creation of a corporate culture which emphasizes innovation from the top down and expects it as a key requirement of its business managers.

The process of evaluating, developing, and commercializing new products has been discussed in a number of publications and invariably the key is strong, integrated team work which has the support and encouragement of top management.

Acquisitions

Corporations acquire other companies or businesses to broaden their product portfolio or to enhance their existing businesses. According to James B. Farley and Edward H. Schwallie of Booz-Allen & Hamilton Inc.,[7] the high rates of acquisition and mergers reflect the combined effects of the following activities:

Low Stock Prices.During the early 1980s, depressed stock prices and price to earning ratios made mergers and acquisitions attractive, provided cash was used in those transactions.

High Inflation.High inflation frequently makes acquiring existing businesses and assets considerably more attractive than the expense and time required for developing new businesses.

Low Growth.The maturing of many industries has provided corporations with large amounts of cash, which both makes acquisitions attractive and by the same token makes corporations with large amounts of cash acquisition candidates.

Foreign Purchasers.Foreign purchasers are attracted to the United States by its large markets, political stability, and strong technology base.

Another observation is the participation of large corporations, which had previously shied away from acquisitions, in some larger mergers and acquisitions. These corporations include General Motors, General Electric, Allied, Monsanto, and DuPont.

Main Elements

A successful acquisition can provide a fast increase in sales and earnings, however, the viability of their future success is questionable. The three main parts in an acquisition or merger are:

- Identification
- Qualification
- Integration

Identification. The responsibility of top management, identification of an acquisition frequently is a strategic move of a major magnitude which will impact the corporation's future. Acquisitions reflect top management's strengths, weaknesses, intuition, confidence, and risk thresholds. Identification may be based on: 1) vertical integration; 2) horizontal diversification; 3) synergistic field from end use markets; 4) synergistic product mix and technology; 5) businesses with strong growth potential; 6) businesses in trouble due to top managements' incompetency, but with a strong potential to become profitable under competent management; and 7) fear of takeover.

Qualification. Once a business with strategic fit has been identified, the second step is *qualification*. Again, this involves diverse functions with technology as one of the major players. The key issues in qualifying an acquisition candidate include:

1. Industry structure - Intensity of competition
2. Financial analysis
3. Technological fit
4. Domestic/International exposure
5. Markets/growth potential/customers
6. Products/growth potential (life cycle)
7. Process technology
8. Margins/Pricing
9. Competitor evaluation
10. Entry/Exit barriers and history
11. Macro factor dependency of markets/products
12. Substitution threats
13. Legal, environmental considerations
14. Management competence

*Integration.*The evaluation of an acquisition consists of both macro and micro factor;, macro factors, however, receive the maximum attention and mainly consist of: financial analysis, the legislative and regulatory environment, and the international environment of business components.

While these factors are extremely important to the attractiveness of an acquisition candidate, they do not address its strategic importance, which was the key criterion for an acquisition in the first place.

The strategic factors to be considered must include a thorough analysis of the acquisition candidate's different product lines, which is as rigorous as the company's internal analysis. If a corporation does not plan and execute strategic management of its own product lines, it is unforeseeable that such an analysis would be conducted on an acquisition candidate. In many cases the internal weaknesses of a corporation are responsible for its problems in a competitive arena, and an acquisition is not likely to solve these problems. An acquisition might seem like a good move on a short-term basis, but if not properly planned, the severity of both managerial and financial problems would increase. The result is divestiture of the acquired company at a price far less than what was initially paid.

The success of an acquisition boils down to how well a corporation is managing its own businesses and whether it has realistically comprehended the magnitude of problems in acquiring and integrating another business with diverse culture, technologies, and markets. This was pointed out in Business Week of April 7, 1986 with General Motors Chairman, Roger B. Smith, having severe problems in integrating GM's and *EDS's* (Electronic Data Systems Corporation) cultures. After GM transferred 10,000 data processing workers and managers to EDS in 1984, Smith had a near revolt on his hands.[8] GM employees were angered over EDS's rigid dress codes and rules of conduct. One GM manager characterized EDS's employee handbook as "something out of a 19th century Presbyterian hymnbook".

Booz-Allen & Hamilton Approach

Consulting companies, particularly those with multiple competencies, can be of great help by providing strong guidance in the field of acquisitions, provided they have full access to the corporation's business portfolio and possess a knowledge of its competencies and constraints.

The acquisition approach used by Booz-Allen and Hamilton Inc.,[7] which has proved to be quite successful, is based on classifying acquisitions based on either business strategy or corporate strategy, followed by strategic evaluation of the acquisition candidate for its value and price and finally pointing out factors that are important in a post acquisition phase.

Based on the experience of Booz-Allen & Hamilton Inc., the process leading to a successful acquisition can be broken down as follows:

Identification
- Mechanical Screening
- "Intelligent" Screening

Qualification
- Stand-Alone Analysis
- Synergy Analysis
- Value and Price

Integration
- Hands-Off Non-related
- Integrated Non-related
- Integrated Related

Regardless of whether an acquisition is made at corporate, sector, or group level, if the strategy of acquisition is not clearly defined, the acquisition will definitely be opportunistic. Sometimes an opportunistic approach works, but more often it does not. Many corporations that did try an opportunistic approach ended up divesting the businesses they acquired.

Many of the corporations lack the resources and expertise required for evaluation of acquisitions, hence the need for a competent consulting company. A consulting company, however, cannot be a substitute for the lack of strategy formulation which must be developed and evaluated by the parent company. The consulting company can provide an experience base and in-depth knowledge.

The Booz-Allen & Hamilton approach of identification follows two steps. First, mechanical screening involves the screening of a group of target companies based on size, location, minimum R.O.A., market to book ratio, etc. The second step, "intelligent" screening, is based on the criteria listed in Table 7.1.

Once the acquisition candidates have been identified, the second step is evaluation. Table 7.2 presents a check list used by Booz-Allen & Hamilton in their evaluation of acquisition candidates. The analysis is conducted both on a stand-alone basis of the target company and by considering the synergistic effects after acquisition. The synergy analysis brings out the value added component resulting from the acquisition candidate.

Category	Strategic Rationale
Business Strategy Based	
• Acquire Synergistic Product Market Niche Position	Achieve scale economies of distribution, production, or technology.
• Acquire Position in Key International Markets	Achieve scale economics for global production and technology investments.
• Acquire a Beachhead in an Emerging High Growth Market	Anticipate high leverage business growth equations by identifying market forcing functions.
• Acquire a Portfolio of Minority Investments in Companies that Represent Homogeneous Businesses.	Apply pressure for improved short-term earnings and sell stock. Gain improved information on future potential.
Corporate Strategy Based	
• Acquire a Company with Underutilized Financial Strength	Use borrowing capacity or other financial strengths, e.g. underutilized tax loss carryforwards or foreign tax credits to achieve an immediate performance premium.
• Acquire an Underskilled Company in a Related Industry	Apply superior marketing, technology, or production expertise to enhance the competitive position and performance of the acquisition candidate.
• Acquire an Underexploited Physical Asset	Anticipate shortages and price increases in the physical asset's value. Invest to exploit the resource using distribution capacity.
• Acquire an Undervalued Corporate Portfolio	Apply more aggressive portfolio management to restructure resource allocation and upgrade results.

Table 7.1   Strategic Approaches to Acquisition[7]
Reprinted with permission.

Often, a strong time pressure in evaluating acquisition candidates calls for an approach to analytical work which is highly efficient, well structured, and concise. This includes the viewpoint of the target company regarding why they should be acquired, an analysis frequently ignored.

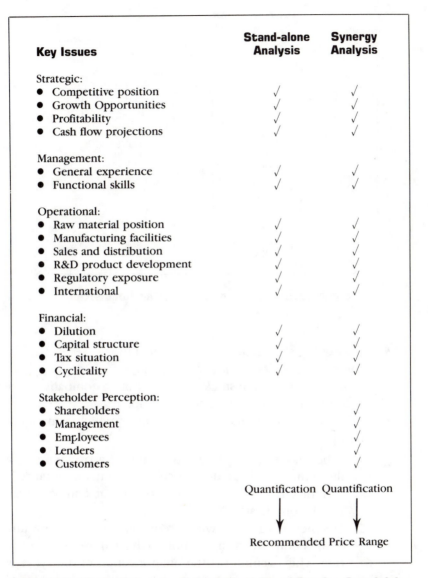

Key Issues	Stand-alone Analysis	Synergy Analysis
Strategic:		
● Competitive position	✓	✓
● Growth Opportunities	✓	✓
● Profitability	✓	✓
● Cash flow projections	✓	✓
Management:		
● General experience	✓	✓
● Functional skills	✓	✓
Operational:		
● Raw material position	✓	✓
● Manufacturing facilities	✓	✓
● Sales and distribution	✓	✓
● R&D product development	✓	✓
● Regulatory exposure	✓	✓
● International	✓	✓
Financial:		
● Dilution	✓	✓
● Capital structure	✓	✓
● Tax situation	✓	✓
● Cyclicality	✓	✓
Stakeholder Perception:		
● Shareholders		✓
● Management		✓
● Employees		✓
● Lenders		✓
● Customers		✓
	Quantification	Quantification
	↓	↓
	Recommended Price Range	

Table 7.2 Case Example of Analytical Checklist for Acquisition Evaluations[7]

Reprinted with permission.

An important part of evaluation is understanding the value and price of the acquisition candidate. Booz-Allen considers the acquisition candidate as having three different values as shown in Figure 7.5.

To determine the value and price of an acquisition, the following key issues should be considered:

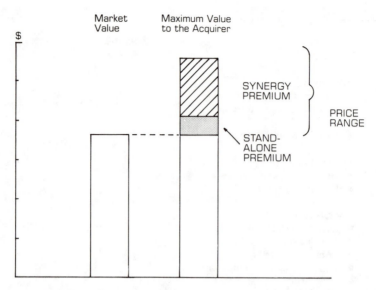

Figure 7.5   Value and Price of an Acquisition[7]
Reprinted with permission.

- the selling shareholders price expectations
- the competing contenders' price range
- *Market Value* — the stock price of a public company or the value to the owner of a private company
- *"The Maximum Value* to the acquirer which consists of two parts:

  1. "The market price adjusted by either a premium or a discount to reflect differences between the acquirer's and the current owner's perception of the company on a stand alone basis.

  2. "A synergy premium which represents the unique value of the company as an addition to the acquirer's organization. This premium is the quantification of the synergy analysis and can include such benefits as economics of scale, savings in administrative costs, joint R&D and advertising programs, etc. When several companies seek the same acquisition, the synergy premium will vary for each contender." (p.37)[7]

- *Purchase Price*, which will be a function of the negotiating skills of the two parties and, in order to be justified, should lie somewhere between the market value and the maximum value.

Post-acquisition Phase

Acquiring a company consists of acquiring assets and an organization, with the intent to generate a return on these assets. The price of acquisition is a function of the expected returns rather than the value of assets alone. This highlights the importance of integrating a new entity into the existing organization. Table 7.3 shows some of the challenges which must be met during the postacquisition phase. Many of these issues will be easier to resolve if they are anticipated during the process leading up to the acquisition.

The success or failure of an acquisition depends upon how well the business and technology of the acquisition can be integrated with

Major Challenges	Hands-Off Non-related Acquisition	Integrated Non-related Acquisition	Integrated Related Acquisition
• Stakeholder perception	✓	✓	✓
• Financial policy	✓	✓	✓
• Capital allocation procedures	✓	✓	✓
• Executive compensation	✓	✓	✓
• Financial control systems	✓	✓	✓
• Budget and planning systems	✓	✓	✓
• Organizational fit		✓	✓
• Administrative systems		✓	✓
• R&D priorities		✓	✓
• "Company culture" issues		✓	✓
• Raw materials and supply management			✓
• Facilities rationalization			✓
• Production flow and inventory systems			✓
• Sales and distribution network			✓

Table 7.3   The Post-Acquisition Phase[7]
Reprinted with permission.

that of the new parent corporations. If the parent corporation is incapable of integrating its own businesses and technology, it is unlikely that an acquisition strategy will succeed in the long run.

SUMMARY

Corporations deploy large amounts of financial and human resources in buying or acquiring businesses and technology, yet pay little attention to their practicality and strategic fit. Strong technology companies buy such resources either to enhance their existing position or to reduce time restraints on internal development. Evaluation and follow through of technological developments is an absolute necessity for success. Technology or business acquisition is almost never as easy as it seems. Analysis reveals that the businesses or technology have been optimized for a different set of environmental parameters from those intended by the purchaser. The cost of customizing businesses or technology should be considered before such acquisitions are carried out.

REFERENCES

1. Smithburg, D.W.: Competitive Leverage, The Conference Board, Report No. 876; p. 3-4, 1985.

2. Welch, J.: "Where is Marketing Now That We Really Need It?", presented to the Conference Board's 1981 Marketing Conference, Grand Hyatt, New York, October 28, 1981.

3. Krugh, L.C.: Seminar on Corporate Development, March 5, 1985.

4. Allen, N., Shaw, J.C., and Simon, H.A.: *Contemporary Approaches to Creative Thinking.* Alberton Press, New York, 1963.

5. Tiep, B.: Generating New Product Ideas. The Conference Board, Report No. 546, 1972, p. 43.

6. Twiss, B.: *Managing Technological Innovation.* Longman, London, 1974, p. 96.

7. Farley, J.B., and Schwallie, E.H.: An Approach Towards Successful Acquisitions. The Texas Business Executive; Booz-Allen & Hamilton, Inc.; Fall/Winter 1981, pp. 32-39.

8. Whiteside, D.E.: Roger Smith's campaign to change the GM culture. *Business Week,* April 7, 1986, p. 84.

MAIN CONSIDERATIONS IN INTEGRATING TECHNOLOGY AND BUSINESS

INTEGRATION OF TECHNOLOGY AND BUSINESS

In a typical business plan, the issues addressed are mostly market and finance related. Technology related issues are often crucial to the short and long term viability of the product line, but are seldom addressed in any depth in the planning process or business plan. These technology issues are normally addressed through the different functions of technology and are handled as problems arise. In many cases the wrong skills and talents are assigned to solve them and they are often addressed at too low an organizational level. Persons assigned this function need to have a perspective considerably broader than the narrowly defined range of the immediate problem to ensure evaluation of all possible alternatives. This is one of technology management's major inefficiencies, and the results are directly reflected in the business profit margins.

With an integrated technology plan, technology issues can be identified before they reach a crisis stage and can be handled in a systematic fashion. Time is then available to ensure that the right mix of skills and talents are assigned to solve the problems. Planning will not prevent future events from happening, but will prepare technology management to handle them in the most cost-effective fashion.

A technology effort alone can rarely have a major impact in gaining market share or increasing profit margins, unless this effort is carried out in concert with the marketing department. By the same token, it is hard to visualize a successful marketing effort without appropriate technology support. A strong interaction between the two will result in: 1) identifying and fulfilling market needs in a cost-effective fashion and, 2) providing a strong integrated competitive force. An integrated technology/marketing effort results in identifying market niches for differentiated and new products, which are developed and produced using the technology base. By itself, neither marketing nor technology can provide any significant competitive advantage to a product line.

An integration of technology and business must include all areas of business which are affected by technology developments. Examples of these are:

- Threat of substitution for existing technology in manufacturing current products
- Obsolescence of current product lines
- Development of products which substitute for or compliment existing products
- Development of new products

The importance of integrating technology and business to a corporation's profitability is well illustrated by a number of failures which have resulted from the lack of such an effort.

- Xerox, once a dominant force in copying machines, losing major market share to Japanese
- Dominance of Japanese in the automobile business
- GE and RCAs multimillion dollar losses in the computer business

Business failures in technology-based industries fall into three categories. First, companies may fail to exploit fully advances in the technologies of their traditional businesses. Second, they may ignore or underrate the competitive threat from new technologies. Third, companies may overestimate the appeal of a new technology and expect markets that do not exist and/or fail to develop. (p.11)[1]

Product Line Evaluation

Numerous instances demonstrate that corporate management needs the best possible tools for anticipating new technology and integrating it with the strategic business planning process.

The first step in the integration of technology and business is to evaluate a product line in its entirety. This evaluation will bring out technology and business issues important to the product line's continued success. In addition, such an exercise initiates a detailed dialogue between technology and market functions, an extremely important part of the integration process.

Key Questions in the evaluation process include:

1. What kind of emphasis should be placed on which product line?
2. What is the extent of resources to be committed in such an effort?
3. What value added benefit is received from this effort?

Answers to the above questions are governed by the nature of a product line and its position in a corporation's business portfolio. A product line which is important to the corporation must be evaluated in its entirety. The results of this analysis are used as the basis for continuing technology support to assure the long term viability of the product line.

In a competitive environment each product line has to be evaluated for its future viability. This evaluation must consider direct and functional substitutions and changing social factors. It must determine: 1) if and when a new technology will overtake a mature one or, 2) when changing social factors alter the balance between modes of satisfying a need. An integrated technology and business plan addresses all aspects of a product line, from raw materials through processing to final products, and includes the product end use markets and technologies. Such an evaluation assures technology/business involvement and cooperation beginning with the initial stages of the planning process and addresses all technology and business issues. The following are important categories and factors to be considered in an evaluation of a product line.

Raw Materials

Raw materials can affect a product line's processing costs and/or product quality, which ultimately impacts markets and profitability. A change in raw material quality can upset processing conditions, yields, product purity, and the products physical nature. These in turn influence customers' processing, products, and profitability. The importance of raw materials is well illustrated in the petro-chemical industry, where a shift in raw material sourcing from domestic sources to the Middle East has affected the structure and competitive position of the whole industry. A focused effort in raw material evaluation assures competitive price and suitable quality. For raw materials which have a single supplier, alternate suppliers or even vertical integration should be considered. The regional location of a supplier will influence the inventory of raw materials. Once such an assessment has been made and a raw material strategy defined, it should be reevaluated on a regular basis (the timing of which depends upon the nature of the raw materials). Such a focused effort on raw material supply should result in projections of future costs and identification of alternate raw materials, incentives for vertical integration, and impacts of processing cost or product quality changes in the raw materials.

The following are some of the important factors in raw material considerations: sources/suppliers/quality; future availability/price; impact of technology on raw material sourcing; transportation and hazards; and storage.

Process

An assessment of raw materials without a thorough knowledge of the process is impossible; the two must be integrated. Ideally, the process and raw material evaluations should be looked at first as if a new plant were to be built, and should include all recent developments in technology pertinent to the process and the impact of any emerging technologies. Elements of new process technology should contribute to improvements in fixed and operating costs and assure safe, environmentally sound operation. The information generated can then be used for determining fixed and operating costs of the "process of the future."

During the last two decades, manufacturing industries have gone through a number of major process changes. These changes were made to reduce energy usage, to satisfy environmental and safety regulations, and to reduce processing costs. To maintain a competitive position, a continued emphasis on process modification based on emerging technologies is a must. All process modifications impact product cost or quality, if not both and may be manifested in one or more of the following areas:

- Raw Material Efficiencies
- Co-product/By-product Ties
- Fixed Cost
- Variable Cost
- Process Technology
- Alternate Processes
- Safety/Environmental
- Wastes

The next question is how the information generated for the "process of future" can be used for the existing manufacturing facility. Segments of the improved process are compared to the existing operation and their impact on fixed and variable costs is evaluated. If there is economic justification, the areas of improvement should be developed and implemented into the existing facility. Such an approach also provides the lead time to develop areas of improvement well in advance of the need. The overall result of raw material and process evaluations, development and implementation should assure a competitive process producing an acceptable product quality at the lowest cost. Since product cost is also a function of volume, no amount of technology superiority can overcome the disadvantage of having a low market share. However, technology superiority can help increase profit margins by lowering the break even cost of a product line.

Product

Manufacturing costs of a product are governed by the costs of raw materials and processing. The product of one company generally becomes a raw material for another company, until the final product is sold to consumers. When the product is used as a raw material by different customers, their concerns include:

- Value in use
- Functional and identical substitutes
- Price/Availability
- Quality
- Storage/Transportation/Distribution
- Safety

In addition to satisfying customers' present needs, it is important to evaluate the cost performance of other functional or identical substitutes which are available or under development.

Markets

Markets receive maximum attention in the business plan. Conceptually, market planning consists of two steps: 1) the selection of particular markets, ie, the customers to whom the company wishes to appeal; and 2) the development of marketing mix or the selection and combination of marketing components that the company wishes to use in identified market needs, ie, product mix or modifications, price, place and promotion. Other factors important in market analysis are: 1) structure of each market; 2) market drivers; 3) product sales pricing by markets; 4) product sales, historical and projected;

5) product life cycle for different market segments; 6) importance of products to customer; and 7) key customer economic power.

The major concerns of a marketing department are market share, pricing strategy, profit margins, and projections about the future growth rates of various market segments. These concerns are overlayed by competitive pressures and substitution threats.

Customers

In an environment of changing raw materials, process technologies, and new products, the customer support area deserves a lot more attention than merely servicing the short term concerns. Customer's needs can be affected by emerging production technologies which provide a competitive edge and may involve the use of different products. Customers are the focal point of many corporations who are competing to supply goods and services. The existing supplier of goods must foresee what future developments can impact their product lines and then make use of the opportunities to minimize threats and maximize competitive position. The truly successful companies know their customers as well or better than the customers know themselves and can often perceive developing needs well ahead of the customer. Some of the important areas in evaluating customer needs are: 1) customers' end-uses; 2) customers' technologies; 3) substitutions - direct and functional; 4) impact on the environment after product is discarded; 5) strategic importance of end use product to the consumer; and 6) growth rates in different market segments.

Competitor Evaluation

In an environment of global competition, it is extremely difficult to know competitors strategies. If they are determined by their market place activities, it is often too late to react other than from a position of weakness. By being proactive in technology/business strategic planning and implementation, one can take optimum advantage of opportunities and minimize the impact of threats.

It is important to know your competitor's strategy, but care should be exercised in allocating resources to this function. Developing a basic set of questions such as, "What do you want to know about competition?" "Why do you want to know about competition?" "How will you get the information?" "What will you do with it?" "Who will do it?" and "At What cost?" is the first step in rational analysis of competition. A sensible approach can be layed out based upon the answers to these questions. The approach should consider some or all of the following points depending upon the nature of the product line:

- Market position and market strategies
- Product-market offerings
- Sales service and customer support levels
- Aggressiveness level
- Product vertical integration
- Potentially new competitors
- Functional substitution possibility
- Entry and exit history
- Profitability/ROI/cash position
- Technologies and development histories
- Manufacturing locations, capacities and expansion strategies

Sources of information about competitor strategy include: annual reports, 10Ks; industrial contacts; consultants; customers; patents; publications, trade fairs, professional meetings; and EPA/OSHA records.

Financial Considerations

This is a control function and indicates the profit or loss contribution of the product line. It identifies the cost components and this information should be used for evaluation of different costs vis-a-vis their contribution to the product lines. This information is a vital tool in identifying and correcting product line inefficiencies. The factors considered are: marketing communications budget, price, cost of goods, cost of sales, profit margin, fixed capital, working capital, administration, services and research expenses.

USE OF TECHNOLOGY FORECASTING (TF)

One way of evaluating the importance of technology developments to various product lines is through technology forecasting, which provides an orderly approach to technology predictions rather than a haphazard set of vague, biased opinions. The interactions of these predictions with the socio-economic environment provides an insight into future trends and identifies opportunities and threats to businesses.

Technology forecasting (TF) was developed in the United States in the late 1940s for two reasons. First, technologies were being developed at a rate faster than they could be used, so a strong effort was needed to determine the new areas of utilization. The second reason was the necessity of developing a number of areas parallel to each other, particularly in the space projects. This meant that components of space crafts were not developed sequentially but simultaneously and on the basis of fairly strict specifications. Such specifications covered performance, structural design, cost and completion date. Technology forecasting techniques were developed to meet these requirements.[1]

Technology forecasting was initiated in the United States public sector to manage a number of complex technology programs directed by National Aeronautics and Space Agency (NASA) and Department of Defense (DoD). In the private sector, the emergence of strategic planning highlighted the need for forecasts.

Barriers

If technology forecasting can accomplish and provide corporations a powerful tool in planning and integrating technology with business, why is it not used extensively?

The initial thrust of technology forecasting was towards the development of quantitative techniques, with little or no emphasis towards real life situations. The result was a range of techniques and extensive literature on the subject. In the late 1970s, technology forecasting emerged as a tool more for new product development, rather than for corporate planning, and combined creativity spurring techniques with those of forecasting. Like strategic business planning, technology forecasting is a way of thinking and the two methodologies share a strong synergism. It is this synergistic effect which can act as a bridge in integrating business and technology. As a matter of fact, these techniques are used extensively in Japan, both by government agencies and private corporations.[2]

The following are some of the barriers in the effective utilization of technology forecasting.

- Language barriers between business, technology, and technology forecasting.
- Aversion to long term planning. This is a carryover from educational training which most corporations make little or no attempt to counteract.

- The threat of goal setting and commitments — a result of planning.
- Need for a strong team interaction between marketing, manufacturing, and R&D — three functions mostly at odds with each other.
- Top management's thrust towards short term objectives rather than a balanced approach between short- and long-term goals.

Advantages

In spite of the above barriers, technology forecasting is being used by a number of corporations such as IBM, Boeing, Alcoa, United Technologies, and many small corporations. It has been used extensively by DoD, NASA, and other government agencies.

Technology forecasting methods by themselves will not identify inventions, opportunities, or threats. These TF methods do assist in accomplishing the following objectives:[3]

1. Project rates of technology substitution.
2. Assist in the management of technical R&D programs.
3. Evaluate present value of technology.
4. Identify and evaluate new products and processes.
5. Analyze value of new technologies to the organization.

Project Rates of Technology Substitution

Replacing existing technology with a new one is extremely important to all organizations. Doing this in a timely and efficient way, however, is often difficult for the company to accomplish mainly because of the complacency of the operating organization. A number of organizations have successfully used TF methods to evaluate the impact of new technology or substitution products on their businesses. This provides the timely information required to develop a strategy for taking the appropriate actions to either utilize it as an opportunity or to counteract its threat. TF methods have been used by the Pilkington Corportion of England to forecast the substitution rate of one thickness of glass for another and the substitution of plastic for glass. (pp.4–5)[3]

Assist in the Management of Technical R&D Programs

If there is no systematic way of formulating R&D programs, one or more of the following occurs: 1) extension of the past work, irrespective of its economic value; 2) revival of old programs; 3) work on perceived threats or opportunities; 4) heavy involvement in the manufacturing and market support areas; 5) projects based upon biased opinions of management; and 6) projects originated due to EPA or OSHA pressure. In other words, R&D does everything except what it is supposed to do — provide a well-focused approach to keep existing businesses competitive and to provide a strong effort for future growth.

TF techniques can provide an unbiased approach to R&D programs through the methodology of evaluating and assessing the competitive forces and by providing an insight to market needs.

Examples of the use of TF techniques in R&D management include Bell Helicopter's use for R&D resource allocation and Boeing's use to evaluate passenger compartment design. (p.6)[3]

Evaluate Present Value of Technology

The key questions concerning the value of any technology under development are:

- Market size, growth, and expected penetration rate.
- Time and cost for commercializing the technology.
- Impact of competing technologies and non-technical factors on the profit potential of the technology under development.

The first question is addressed by evaluating the needs that will be served by the technology under development and a study of the historic takeover rates of new technologies. The second question is addressed by analyzing the past development of similar technologies and identifying the areas of development that will require a major breakthrough for the technology to be economically viable. The third question deals with identifying competing technologies either in use or under development and an assessment of non-technical factors such as environmental, social, political, regulatory, and economic that might impact the attractiveness of the technology under development. (p.7)[3]

Identify and Evaluate New Products and Processes

Most organizations are more concerned about competitive products or processes than identification of new opportunities because the failure to identify and capitalize on new opportunities seems unrelated to the well being of existing businesses. In reality the two are closely related and a well-designed technology forecasting program should address both areas.

Some examples of corporations who have used technology forecasting for the identification of new business opportunities are: (p.8)[3]

Whirlpool — new household appliances.
New York Telephone Company and IBM — new product needs.
Owens-Corning Fiberglass — products and processes.
ALCOA — threats to existing markets; new business areas.

Analyze Value of New Technologies to the Organization

Any major changes in suppliers' and/or customers' technologies can have a strong impact on the technology posture of the organization. If recognized well in advance, they can provide numerous opportunities, if ignored or not recognized at all, they result not only in the loss of opportunity, but also as a threat to existing products and processes. In such instances, TF methods can help identify these opportunities and/or threats so that an organization can be well prepared to handle these situations before they reach a crisis stage. This advanced information helps in planning for the training and development needs of the organization's work force.

Companies who have used technology forecasting in this way include:

- The Western Corporation who has used TF methods to assist in work force planning.
- The Weyerhauser Corporation who is using TF methods to determine future technical personnel requirements for their information system.
- The U.S. Navy Underwater Science Center who has used TF techniques in analyzing the effectiveness of its R&D organization. and
- Union Carbide who uses TF methods to improve utilization of personnel. (pp.9–10)[3]

SUMMARY

Technology forecasting is based on a number of observations connected with technological developments. The first is technological escalation. When the performance of a technology development is plotted against time, it is often found to be an S-Shaped curve which reflects that the development of new technology gets underway as soon as a number of bottlenecks are removed, indicated by the slow progress of technology development in the initial phases. Once these bottlenecks are removed, technology progress becomes exponential due to experience curve effects. Every technology has limits to its performance ceiling, which is relfected by a reverse S curve. It is often observed that when a technology has reached its performance limit, a new technology is developed with a higher ceiling. The development of this technology also follows an S curve. These curves often cross, ie, by the time one technology has reached its ceiling, the new technological developments are already in progress.

Frequently, social changes stimulate technological development through pressures exerted by political and legal systems. Such has been the case for all the technologies developed to control environmental emissions during the 1970s.

The key premises of technology forecasting are based on the fact that science builds on science and technology builds on technology, except for rare random discoveries. Technological developments often cast their shadows a long time before they appear, although often only in scientific journals and patent abstracts. One can identify what new technologies are at what stage of development and by whom they are being developed. Successful utilization of technology forecasting combines elements of scientific discovery with market need and projects what technological developments are necessary to meet that market need.

The recognition and evaluation of technology forecasts and market needs are of limited value unless they stimulate a managerial response. "The type of response can take several forms, largely depending upon the magnitude of the impact of the forecast development and the confidence that can be placed in the information. On some occasions where a major threat or opportunity to the business as a whole is discovered, diversification or merger may be the appropriate course to take. In such cases the contribution of forecasting will have been to enable the organization to anticipate events and take timely action from a position of strength. At a level where only part of a business is affected, new R&D programs may be initiated or emphasis changed. A longer term change may be anticipated and addressed by recruiting and building up an R&D team with an expertise new to the company" (p.12)[1] or acquisition of a specialized company to strengthen the area of anticipated threat or opportunity.

In certain cases, a major potential threat is revealed but is dependent upon a breakthrough in a particular field of technology. This points to an area which needs to be watched closely and monitored to give early warning.

The methodology of technology forecasting is very similar to strategic business planning and consists of both macro and micro factors. At the macro level they relate to broad external events such as sociological, political, economic and technological indicators at both national and international levels. At the micro level, the concerns involve emerging technologies that might affect the industry, markets, products, processes, and competition. These areas of information are analyzed based upon the past, present, and anticipated future. It is in the latter area that forecasting can provide a sense of the expected future in which the organization will function and on the basis of which it will discover its opportunities and make decisions on its objectives, strategies, and action programs to produce appropriate strategic plans. (p.19)[1]

Since the future is an extension of past through present, all planning must be based on an extensive knowledge of the present. The true benefit of technology forecasting comes from considering both "technology push" and "market pull." Innovations occur when technology capacity is matched with a need of society, be it for the consumer (products and services), the organization as an operator (equipment and process), or society as a whole (environmental protection, defense, and health). The technological capability must be able to support the level of investment required to satisfy the need.

The planning process should:

- Forecast the states of relevant technological development within a required time frame.
- Evaluate the cost of partaking in those developments.
- Assess the economic benefits to the organization for making the investment - which entails, the probable magnitude of the market, and its growth rate. (p.34)[1]

The technology forecast is only one of the inputs to the planning process. To be useful, the forecast must be translated into a threat or opportunity to the corporation. This significance must be assessed by the profit or loss impact to the business.

REFERENCES

1. Jones, H., Twiss, B.C.: *Forecasting Technology for Planning Decisions*. PBI, New York, 1978.
2. Irvine, J., Martin, B.R.: *Foresight in Science*. Frances Pinter, Dover, N.H., pp. 107-132.
3. Vanston, J.H.: Technology Forecastings . . . An Aid to Effective Technology Management, Technology Futures Inc. Austine, Texas.

TECHNOLOGY AND TECHNOLOGY FORECASTING TECHNIQUES

TECHNOLOGY AND ITS EVALUATION

Technology forecasting can be better understood by considering separately its two components: technology and forecasting.

Three experts in the field of technology forecasting define technology as follows:

Technology consists of three elements: 1) the physical things — tools, machines, and materials that mankind uses for all activities, 2) the software aspects of technology including technical processes and procedures such as heat treating sequences, computer programs, operations research techniques, and the Federal Aviation Administration's (FAA) traffic control system for civil aviation, and 3) definitional systems that determine and describe the foregoing such as Society of Automotive Engineers (SAE) standards for motor oil, National Electrical Manufacturers Association (NEMA) standards for electric motor insulation, and standards for screw threads. Then the definition of technology becomes troublesome. Is the social security program a technology? The welfare program? Our money system? These things are called social technology. Thus, the definition excludes these procedures to direct social activity and applies only to technical devices and activities.[1]

James R. Bright
Technology Futures, Inc.

Technology is the systematic application of organized knowledge to practical activities, especially productive ones.[1]

John H. Vanston
Technology Futures, Inc.

Technology is products, processes, tools and devices, and their organization for use by people in fashioning the goods and services that constitute their environment.[2]

Gary S. Stacey
Battelle Memorial Institute
Columbus, Ohio

Each one of these definitions implicitly or explicitly defines technology in terms of goods and services that relate to people. In addition, each defines technology to include the form of management of a business or the organization of a production line. Though the organizational form may change from one business to another or from one production process to another, the technical components remain the same. Finally, by these definitions, all technology serves to improve the delivery or use of goods and services, which is after all, the role of business. When this role is carried out responsively and efficiently, the business serves its markets, earns profits, and ensures its long-term viability.

In addition to the business issues just discussed, the successful utilization of technology is also based on the economic circumstances within which the technology itself is likely to be developed. The demand for processes and products, capital availability, interest rates, profitability, and overall economic conditions strongly influence the rate of replacement of old and adoption of new technologies.

Technology Forecasting

The following is a brief description of Technology Forecasting which has been obtained and reproduced from Gary S. Stacey's work at Battelle Memorial Institute, Columbus, Ohio (pp.4–7).[2]

Historically, it has been found that when the performance of a technology is plotted against time, it takes the form of an S curve as shown in Figure 9.1. Initially, the performance (miles per hour or horse power per cubic inch) for a technology (like an airplane or an

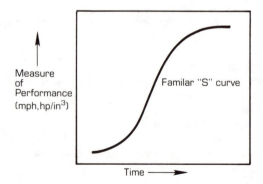

Figure 9.1 The "S" curve of technological performance over time

internal combustion engine) increases slowly. In the middle range, the technology is better understood and applied, and the performance increases more rapidly as the technology reaches its most well developed shape. Then, as the technology matures, performance increases taper off. This observation forms the basis of some of the TF techniques.

This relationship is valuable for predicting technology's expected rate of application to problems and for comparing the performance of one technology with another. A series of S curves, one on top of the other, as shown in Figure 9.2, illustrates technological change and the replacement of one technology by another over time.

From a business view, certain aspects of a technology are especially pertinent:

1. the reasons for its conception and development
2. barriers to its development
3. its connection to economics and markets
4. its timeframe - existing, key, or emerging.

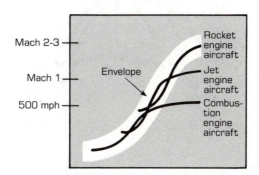

Figure 9.2   The "envelope" curve of S curves

Reasons for a Technology's Conception and Development

In business, a technology does not exist in the abstract. Instead, it is developed and applied to satisfy a market need or resource constraint. As shown in Figure 9.3, the purpose of or requirements for technology are primarily driven by market needs and resource constraints. The need for innovation in business usually provides and guides the underlying stimulus for identifying and developing new technologies and applying them in production processes and products.

For example, the market need for improved vision led to the development of eyeglasses and subsequently the replacement technology of contact lenses. Further refinement of that technology is now occurring as soft contact lenses replace hard lenses. Another example is resource constraints. The reduced availability or vastly inflated costs of petroleum or automobile fuel, have provided the incentive for developing products that will reduce petroleum consumption. The resource constraint, therefore, has created the need for developing new technologies used in the final product, automobiles.

However, as the figure also suggests, the development of technologies is not always driven by market needs. In some cases, market needs arise from the discovery and application of new technologies. Technology can create demand for itself as exemplified by electronic games. The demand for PAC-MAN would not have occurred without the development of computer microprocessor technology.

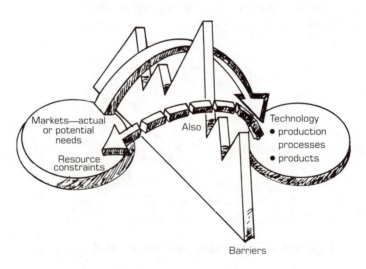

Figure 9.3   Technology Drivers[2] *Reprinted with permission.*

Barriers to Technological Development

A variety of barriers inhibit the flow of information relating society, its market needs, and resource constraints to the demands for technology in production processes and products. As a result, accurate identification of market needs and resource constraints is difficult, and technological development is impeded. The primary barriers relate to laws, social values, resource constraints, and time. While an archaic law requiring that a pedestrian carrying a lantern precede any horseless carriage moving through a town in New England did not prevent the development and ultimate use of the automobile, other less ludicrous laws of this type can inhibit development. For example, current U.S. laws constrain branch banking services. Copyright and patent laws affect the development and use of video cassette and disc technology. Such laws impact — in different ways and degrees — the growth and development of technologies for use both in manufacturing and in products.

Changes and differences in societal values and tastes can also erect barriers to selecting the most appropriate technology to serve the needs of specific groups. Understanding those values and tastes, including the differences among them, is important in deciding which technologies are most applicable to meeting the market needs of different groups. In the United States, the influence of those who object to nuclear power plants is an example of how strong a factor values and tastes can be.

Many possible technologies could be applied to meeting market demands and overcoming resource constraints, if only sufficient funds were available to effect their full development. Funding is also required to test, modify, and ultimately make the technologies applicable for production and for use in final products. Resource constraints — like limits on the availability of capital, properly trained personnel, and other material inputs — affect the rate of technological change and development. Because perfect information is not available on future market requirements or their potential resource constraints, estimates on the rate of development of a technology and its likely application are never free of uncertainty. However, this information gap can be better bridged by acknowledging that resource and knowledge barriers do exist and then seeking well-rounded forecasts of the needs and constraints — whether regional, national, or international in scope — that various groups and markets face.

Technology's Relation to Time

The final complicating factor in understanding technology and its relationship to markets is time. The present relationship between technologies and markets is very complex and difficult to understand. Nevertheless, companies invest in R&D and other strategic technologies in the hope of future payoffs. Decisions anticipating future events must consider the timing of changes in social and economic needs, the timing of the development of technologies to address those needs, and the effect of barriers and facilitators on the length of time to ultimate use. These effects must be forecast either explicitly or implicitly in strategic and R&D decision making. Technological forecasting can help determine the appropriate timing for R&D and other investments by, for example, helping to establish when and how rapidly an existing product or process will be superseded by another technology.

As illustrated in Figure 9.4, technologies may be characterized as existing, key, or emerging. Instead of measuring the technology in terms of its total performance on the vertical axis, the technology in this figure is measured in terms of the sales of products or the production levels attained. The horizontal axis represents time with the vertical line labeled "now" representing the present. The broken lines on the curve show uncertainty of future trends and the range of possible development, illustrating the need for reliable technological forecasts.

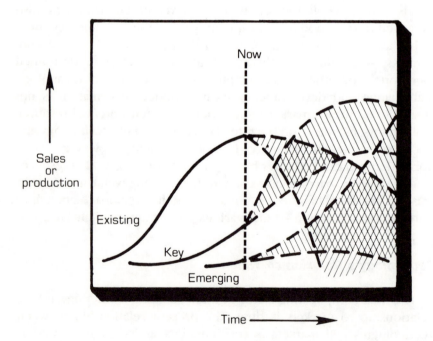

Figure 9.4   Characteristics of Technological Development[2]

Note that the S-shaped curve forms the fundamental basis for the relationship between time and the level of sales or production associated with the technology. In this illustration, however, the curve representing the technology peaks and eventually declines when its use in products or production declines. This happens if: 1) the product or process using the technology is no longer in demand; or 2) the product or production process is replaced by an alternative, more efficient, cost-saving technology.

All existing technologies, even those with well-developed applications in wide use, are threatened by alternative technologies and by changing market needs. Key technologies pose the greatest and most immediate threat: Their development and use largely determine the remaining life and expected marketplace for existing technologies. If a competing key technology gains rapidly in sales or production, use of the existing technology drops quickly. On the other hand, if barriers to a key technology cause its use to increase very slowly, sales and production of the existing technology will not drop as quickly.

Emerging technologies are usually known and recognized in the current time period and are candidates for replacing existing and key technologies. Although they may grow rapidly and eventually replace a key technology, however, they may also, after experimentation and investigation, disappear altogether. They have not reached the same level of development, demonstration, and application as the key technologies. The key technology is very likely to replace an existing technology; the main question is, how quickly? The emerging technology, on the other hand, may very well die out. The flying wing is a classic case of an emerging technology that never made it. At one time, it was considered a prime candidate to replace existing bombers because of its substantially improved payload and efficiency. However, subsequent investigation and testing demonstrated a crucial flaw in its overall aerodynamic stability and the technology was abandoned.

An example of existing technology is the use of chemical insecticides to combat crop losses. A candidate key technology corresponding to insecticides is the use of microbial insecticides. The rate at which microbial insecticides replace chemical insecticides will be determined by a variety of factors relating to cost efficiency, as well as to social and political acceptance. An emerging technology to replace microbial insecticides as a method for improving plant yield might be production of an insect-resistant plant form through genetics research. At present, plant genetic solutions to insect resistance are experimental and not well developed, but this approach could ultimately prove superior to both chemical and microbial insecticides.

Obviously, if a company can forecast which emerging technologies will prove commercially feasible and when key technologies will overtake existing technologies, it will be able to enhance its position in the marketplace. This logically brings us to the second component of technology forecasting.

Forecasting

Many methods and a wide variety of tools and techniques are available for forecasting future conditions. The main concept central to producing and using forecasts is that all forecasting is conjecture concerning the future.

Forecasts are made for either the short, medium, or long run. In short-run forecasts, one year or less, technologies are not expected to change substantially. As a general rule, a short-run forecast will deal with a single technology or set of technologies.

The medium-run forecast usually covers a 2- to 10-year period. Because the key technologies are already known, an accurate and reliable view of this timeframe requires forecasts of their rate of use and adoption. Understanding the potential for key technologies will help the decision maker determine not only the most likely outcome for the future, but also the uncertainty that underlies the future business environment.[3]

The long-run forecast, made for a period of 10- to 20-years — a time horizon long enough for new technologies to emerge — must take into account existing, key and emerging technologies, their potential interrelationships, and the wide range of uncertainty implicit in the forecast.

Technological Forecasting: Definition and Procedures

Bringing the terms technology and forecasting together, Stacey defines technological forecasting as "methods for identifying technologies and providing information on alternative future views of their relationship to business; and for forecasting their development, use, and application for new, modified, or improved production or products."[4]

Technological forecasting involves: collecting information, organizing and processing that information, and delivering alternative future views.

Both quantitative and qualitative data need to be collected and organized in a technological forecast. The qualitative data are potentially more important than the quantitative data for understanding how a technology is likely to evolve. These qualitative data can come from a variety of sources, including the judgment of scientists and company experts and information in the open literature.

Mechanisms for organizing, processing and interrelating the data and several models of technological change and replacement are available. (p.7)[2] These form the basis for the technological forecasts, which offer alternative views of how the technology might be applied. These views are important because they reflect the full range of uncertainty relating to the development of the technology.

Rationales for Technology Forecasting

The following definition and brief description of technology forecasting techniques are obtained and reproduced from a technology forecasting course given by Technology Futures, Inc. This brief description is meant to convey an idea of overall concepts rather than details of how to apply these techniques for practical applications. To obtain a detailed working knowledge of these techniques, the reader is encouraged to take the five-day course.[1]

James R. Bright suggests three main rationales for technology forecasting.

The first rationale is that technological capabilities (meaning such qualities as strength, power, speed, size, abrasion resistance, etc.) usually grow in an orderly manner over time or through practice. There is a consistency or pattern in technological changes, and abrupt major deviations are not common. Historical consistency thus provides a basis for a forecast through trend extrapolation.

The second rationale is that technology responds to needs, to opportunities, and to the provision of resources. If these casual forces can be identified, then the technological progress can be anticipated as a response to their pressure and support. Years ago, this rationale may have seemed a bit hypothetical. However, it has increasing validity because of a growing public willingness to use national resources to support the technology leading to desirable social goals. The growing interest in technology assessment is likely a signal of further political and social influence on the character of new technology.

The third rationale is that new technology can be forecast through studying the process of technological innovation — a process taking time that is measured in years and decades. Coming technology casts its shadows far ahead, and signals of emerging technological innovation can be identified and monitored, ultimately providing the basis of a forecast.[1]

According to John H. Vanston:

Technology forecasting describes a group of techniques that predict in quantifiable terms the direction, character, rate, implications, and impacts of technical advance. TF techniques are based on the logical treatment of credible data and should produce results that are both informative and independent of the analyst performing the forecast. Although TFs can serve as effective devices for communication of ideas or for gaining insight on technical progress, they are primarily conducted to provide information to assist planners and managers in making better decisions.[1]

TECHNOLOGY FORECASTING TECHNIQUES

There are 10 to 20 widely used technology forecasting techniques. These techniques can be classified in four major categories:

1. Surveillance
2. Projective
3. Normative (goal oriented)
4. Integrative.

The principles and approach used in each one of the above forecasting techniques are different. In some cases one technique can be classified in more than one category; Delphi Surveys, for example, can be used for projecting future developments, to identify goals, or to integrate the goals of other forecasts.

The following discussion of forecasting techniques is reprinted with permission from John H. Vanston.[5]

Surveillance Techniques

Surveillance techniques can be classified as scanning, monitoring and tracking. These techniques involve search and evaluation of the information; however, the degree of focus and its intensity varies depending upon the technique. Although the tasks involved overlap each other, the skills and talents required to accomplish these techniques can vary widely.

The surveillance techniques are based on two basic observations.

● Most successful innovations go through similar stages of developments, which begin with idea generation and end with widespread adoption.

- There is a large time interval between each stage of development, particularly in the early stages.

In general, surveillance techniques are easy to initiate, amenable to organizational needs, compatible with other organizational activities, and are a must for most of the technology forecasting activities.

All surveillance techniques are essentially passive or observational techniques. In many ways, they are similar, differing primarily in the degree of focus and intensity of the information search effort. Although application of the three techniques may overlap and the same people may be involved in all three simultaneously, it is desirable to keep in mind the different nature of each technique, as noted here.

1. Scanning. This term is applied to broadly oriented surveillance activities which seek to identify, at an early time, developments in technical, economic, social, political, and ecological environments that may materially affect the organization. Scanning programs are particularly useful in identifying emerging products and processes that provide commercial advantage to the organization or its competitors, in pointing out new uses for present or developing technologies, and in suggesting socio-political factors that impede or enhance acceptance of new technologies.

2. Monitoring. Monitoring implies a more focused and disciplined type of surveillance effort than scanning. An effective monitoring plan should include five basic elements: 1) a system for selecting areas to be monitored; 2) a system for assigning specific monitoring responsibilities to individuals or groups; 3) an assessment of progress levels at which developments will become significant to the organization; 4) a clear definition of the action the responsible agent is to take when progress reaches the designated level of importance; and 5) a formal procedure for periodically reviewing the monitoring program and related data bases.

3. Tracking. This is the most carefully focused and intensive of the surveillance techniques. It involves a very concentrated effort to follow developments of major significance to the organization: competitive response to a new product or process nearing introduction; possible near-term introduction of new products and processes that will threaten present markets; major technical breakthroughs in which the organization needs to establish a position. Often, special *ad hoc* groups are organized to conduct or supervise specific tracking efforts.

Projective Techniques

Projective techniques are based on the theory that the past is an indication of the future, at least for some period of time. It assumes that as long as socio-economic forces of the past do not change significantly, past patterns of change will continue in the future. Thus, if the forecaster can understand the past, the future development patterns can be identified. The projective TFs are based on the past experience, modified by an evaluation of how the future may differ from the past.

The 5 projective techniques are described below and can be classified in the following categories: technical trend extrapolation; Pearl curve; precursor developments; substitution analysis; and expert opinion. Three types of expert opinon include: the Delphi Survey, structured interview, and nominal group conferencing.

1. Technical Trend Extrapolation. A large body of empirical data indicates that when the values of key parameters of technical progress are plotted against time, a regular development pattern can be discerned. In a large number of technical areas, it has been found that if progress is plotted against time, the trace is linear on semilog graph for a significant portion of the development period. These projections can be very useful in setting organizational R&D goals, in estimating the progress that may be taking place outside the organization, and in identifying the need for new technical approaches.

2. Pearl Curve. As a technology matures, it will almost invariably begin to approach limits to its development. These limits may be either real or perceived. As a limit is approached, exponential improvement is slowed; thus, it is often useful to know how the limit will be approached. In may cases, it has been found that technical progress in this part of the development period can be approximated by the Pearl formula:

$$y = \frac{L}{1 + a \exp(-bt)}$$

Where, y = value of the parameter at time t, L = parameter limit, and a and b are constants determined from known data.

3. Precursor Developments. It has been observed over a period of years that technical development in one area follows development in other areas in a predictable manner. When such lead-lag relations exist, it is often possible to forecast developments in the lagging technical area by observing the state of development in the leading one. Where progress in the leading technology can also be forecast, this allows reasonable extension of the forecasts' time horizon for the lagging technology.

4. Substitution Analysis. When a given technology begins to mature (ie, as improvements become increasingly difficult and expensive), a new technology will often emerge that can accomplish the required function in a more effective and economic manner. Development of the new technology will allow it to take over progressively larger segments of the market. Analysis of this substitution phenomenon indicates a general pattern to this process, and a number of TF practitioners have described it in mathematical terms. One of the more successful of these attempts was a substitution formula developed by John Fisher and Robert Pry:[6]

$$\frac{f}{1-f} = a \exp(bt)$$

Where, f = degree of substitution at time t, and a and b are empirically derived constants. This formula has been found to roughly describe substitution histories in a number of technical developments in a wide variety of fields. When used for forecasting purposes, one can use early substitution data to determine constants and then project the fraction of market takeover at any time in the future.

5. Expert Opinion. In an ongoing, technically-oriented company, there resides a reservoir of technical talent, experience, and training — scientists, engineers, salespeople, technicians, etc. A well-formulated technology forecasting program will take advantage of the knowledge and wisdom of this collection of experts.

- The Delphi procedure[7] involves four specific rounds. In the first round, the experts are asked to estimate when they expect each of a number of events to occur. When answers are received they are tabulated and, in Round 2, sent to respondents who are requested to reconsider their original projections. Respondents whose Round 2 answers fall in the upper or lower Round 1 quartiles are requested to provide reasons for their estimates. In the third round, respondents are sent the retabulated totals, together with the nonattributed comments gathered in Round 2. Respondents are requested to once again consider their previous projections and are invited to add comments, if desired. For the final round, the person conducting the survey tabulates and distributes all projections and comments. The results of a Delphi survey may be useful in a number of ways. The mean value of estimates gives a projection of when a given technical development may be expected to occur, while the spread of these values can give an indication of the degree of agreement between experts. The survey may also be used to compare the estimates of one group of participants with other groups.

- The structured interview technique is conceptually very similar to the Delphi survey. In this technique, the person conducting the survey personally collects data and acts as an intermediary of ideas. As opposed to procedures for free-form interviews, subject introduction techniques, sequence and nature of questions, discussion procedures, and all administrative details are standardized prior to initiation of the project. The interviewer goes from one participant to the next and adds each interview's results to the data base for the next interview. When all the interviews have been conducted, feedback is normally completed by telephone or written communication with earlier participants.

- Nominal group conferencing[8] is designed to improve the use of expert opinion. It is most effective when a small panel of experts, five to seven, are available for approximately one-half day.

    Experience has shown that nominal group conferencing can be a very useful tool for eliciting potential and imaginative ideas from a group of experts. The method almost assures that all members actively participate in the conference and minimizes many of the social dynamic problems associated with committee meetings. Often, it is useful to conduct a series of nominal group sessions on the same subject matter and analyze differences and similarities in results.

Normative Techniques (Goal Oriented Forecasting)

While projective techniques are based on understanding the past, normative techniques are based on the assumption that future technology developments will be driven by socio-economic needs. It assumes that as future needs are perceived, government and society will provide funds and technical skills to support the development of technologies required to satisfy those needs. Thus, if one can identify the future needs of society in 5, 10, or 20 years, one can forecast the technological needs of the future. The future needs of society depend upon the value system of the society at that time which is likely to be quite different than the existing value system. In addition, the future needs could be numerous with multiple means of being satisfied. The number of needs that can be identified will normally far outmatch the number of technical development programs that any organization can undertake. Thus, the practical use of Normative forecasting involves three tasks: identifying social needs; identifying technologies that will satisfy those needs; and selecting the development of those new technologies that best coincide with an organization's goals, capabilities, and competitive status.

The following techniques are used to accomplish the above tasks:

1. impact wheel.
2. morphological analysis.
3. relevance trees.

1. Impact Wheel. This is a technique for using an informed panel to identify higher order, often non-obvious, impacts and implications of selected decisions or developments. Use of the technique starts with specification of an event, trend, technical advance, or societal development that one wishes to analyze. The panel is then asked to identify the direct consequences of the occurrence of this central item. Once five to seven direct consequences are identified, the panel is asked to suggest possible implications that might arise from each of these first order consequences. This process is continued for third and higher order consequences to the extent that it is useful. Experience has shown that this technique can be a very potent means of identifying unexpected or easily overlooked opportunities, problems, and interrelationships.

2. Morphological Analysis. Most new technologies grow out of a desire to perform some technical function more efficiently or economically. However, in most modern equipment and systems, many subordinate functions are involved in the accomplishment of the overall function. In morphological analysis, the forecaster determines what the major subordinate functions are; identifies the methods that are being used in present systems to accomplish those functions; and examines different ways of combining the subordinate technologies to suggest innovative approaches to accomplishing the basic functions of the overall system. Experience has shown that this technique is quite useful in spurring imaginative ideas about new ways of meeting both existing and postulated future needs. It can also be a valuable device for defensive forecasting (ie, for providing insights into competing products or processes that might be under development).

3. Relevance Trees. For the results of a normative forecast to be applied, the organization must select those technologies which coincide with its objectives and capabilities. One device for assistance in this selection process is the relevance tree technique. The basic principles of this methodology is the division of the relevant elements of a decision into increasingly smaller components; the establishment of formal criteria for specifying the relative importance of each component; the assignment of numerical values for each component and criterion; the quantitative rates of alternate technical solutions against each criterion and component; and the combination of individual ratings to give new insights on the overall decision.

Both the advantages and disadvantages of the method lie in its simplicity. Often, the most important outcome of relevance tree application is the clarification of relationships between factors and the identification of areas requiring more careful study.

Integrative Techniques

The technology forecasting techniques under the categories of surveillance, projective and normative involve projection of developments in a single technology or a small group of technologies. It is obvious that technical developments take place in an interactive environment, where a development in one technology can trigger or accelerate advances in other technologies. Such has been the case in the development of jet engines, which were made practical by advances in metallurgy; computer developments were an outcome of transistors, and later, integrated circuits. Technical advance is often enhanced or hindered by non-technical factors: the technologies for cleaning air and water emissions were developed for chemical and related industries; the reduction in automobile size was triggered by increased oil prices. Thus, forecasts about the future development of a technology must not only take other technical and non-technical developments into account, but also must specify these relationships.

Three technology forecasting techniques can be used to evaluate the interaction of different factors and their impact on new technologies being considered for development.

1. cross impact analysis.
2. scenarios.
3. mathematical models.

1. Cross-impact Analysis.Although all technology forecasting methods are implicitly aware of exogenous influences, it is necessary, on occasion, to address these influences explicitly. One method for taking formal account of such interactive effects is the cross-impact analysis technique. Typically, such analyses begin with an identification of those factors which will most significantly affect the technical development being considered or which will be most affected by the development. These effects might include a change in the probability or significance of the development. Once the factors to be considered are determined, they are arranged in a matrix format with the basic technical development and the other factors arranged in the left hand column and the same arrangement used to form an equal number of columns at the top. The people conducting the analysis complete the matrix by placing in each box a notation of the effect of the occurrence of each element in the left hand column on each of the other elements of the matrix.

In order to simultaneously consider a large number of interactions, mathematical formulas relating events are often developed. With appropriate input data, these formulas result in projections which take into account all included factors. Since solution of the relevant equations may be difficult, computers are often used.

Cross-impact analysis can be a very effective method for examining the probability that a technical development will be affected by exogenous factors. Thus, it can provide a basis for a targeted surveillance program.

2. Scenarios.One method of examining and presenting the interactions between projections of a number of technical and nontechnical factors is to combine them into an integrated description of the future.[9] Such descriptions are often referred to as "scenarios" and are quite useful in technology planning. Since a scenario presents a multifaceted portrait of the future, it allows more realistic consideration of "real world" situations and adds both breadth and depth to decisions about future operations. Moreover, because of its "story" orientation, it often allows the organization to consider alternative futures in a serious, but non-threatening manner.

The use of alternate scenarios in planning can involve considerable expenditure of time and effort. However, experience has shown that the technique illustrates for planners the importance of flexible planning, serves as an excellent interorganizational communication tool, provides a vehicle for integrating relevant technical and non-technical factors in the planning process, provides a basis for an effective monitoring plan, and identifies important decisions that will have to be made in the future.

3. Mathematical Models.Application of most of the technology forecasting methods described above can be abetted by the use of simple mathematical models. It is also beneficial to utilize the power of modern computers to integrate a number of technical and non-technical projections and to take into account the interactions between them. Use of appropriate mathematical models and computer simulations may allow the consideration of many more factors than might otherwise be possible and may also permit the planner to test the implications of different organizational programs and strategies.

4. Partitive Analytical Forecasting.In this model, all tasks necessary for product introduction are identified, different methods for accomplishing these tasks are determined, and the relationship between tasks and means of accomplishment is integrated into a development logic network similar to a PERT network.[10,11] Estimates of the time necessary to complete each task and the probability of complete or partial task completion are determined using expert opinion, past experience, or trend analysis. Finally, computer simulation is used to determine the probability of product development success as a function of time.

SUMMARY

Technology forecasting can play a strong role in the strategic management of technology. However, it must be recognized that its formal institution within an organization must be phased in gradually. This is a lesson learned from strategic planning of business, which took on the average 3 to 5 years to be implemented within corporations. It must be recognized at the onset that technology forecasting techniques overlap the strategic business planning process and could meet a strong resistance from the business planners. Thus, it is extremely important for the planning department to be exposed to TF in the early stages of its initiation. Another risk of TF is that its quantitative techniques, while powerful, could distract from objective analysis of future needs through mathematical manipulation. A well-balanced TF approach must be objective and subjective in its application.

The following steps are recommended for establishing a technology forecasting program.

1. Examine technological history of the organization.
2. Determine proper role for technology forecasting in organization.
3. Organize and train core forecasting group.
4. Conduct and evaluate several limited scope forecasts.
5. Expand forecasting activities within the organization.

The key to successful technology forecasting involves an appreciation of the holistic environment in which technology operates and consists of social, political, economic, environmental, ecological, technological, and competitive forces. Any attempt made in technology forecasting without considering the impact of the above factors is likely to be of limited value. This clearly points to the need for a number of inputs in the process of technology forecasting, whose magnitudes will vary depending upon whether technology forecasting is for short, medium, or long-term purposes.

REFERENCES

1. Technology Futures, Inc. 411 West 13th Street, Austin, Tx 78701.

2. Stacey, G.S.: Battelle Technical Inputs to Planning. Review No. 14, 1984. Battelle Memorial Institute, Columbus, Ohio.

3. Martino, J.P.: *Technological Forecasting for Decision Making;* (ed. 2). North Holland, NY, 1983.

4. Stacey, G.S.: Using technology forecasting for R&D and strategic planning. International Congress of Technology and Technology Exchange. Pittsburgh, Oct. 10, 1984.

5. Vanston, J.H.: *The Use of Technology Forecasting in Coordinating New Product Development and Market Evaluation.* Technology Futures, Inc., Austin, TX, 1986.

6. Fisher, J.C., and Pry, R.R.: A Simple Substitution Model of Technological Change, Report No.70-C-215, General Electric Company, Schenectady, NY, 1970.

7. Linstone, H.A., Turoff, M. (eds): *The Delphi Method Techniques and Applications.* Addison-Wesley, Reading, MA, 1975.

8. Delbec, A.L., Van de Ven, A.H., Gustafson, D.H.: *Group Techniques for Program Planning.* Scott-Foresman, Glenview, IL, 1975.

9. Vanston, J.H.: Alternate scenario planning. *Technology Forecasting and Social Change* 10, 1977, 159-180.

10. Vanston, J.H.: PAF - A new probabilistic, computer-based technique for technology forecasting. *Technology Forecasting and Social Change* 10: 239-258, 1977.

11. Honton, E.J., Stacey, G.S., Millett, S.M.: Future Scenarios: The Basic Computational Method. Economics and Policy Analysis Occasional Paper Number 44; Battelle, Columbus, Ohio.

INTEGRATION OF TECHNOLOGY AND BUSINESS AT THE CORPORATE LEVEL

1234567890

EXISTING STATUS

Corporations are currently limited in their capability to exploit to its fullest technology for competitive advantage. This problem arises because CEOs and VPs of technology do not understand how they can communicate with each other in order to fully integrate technology with corporate objectives.

Efforts to integrate business and technology must stem from the senior corporate management level. The VP-technology must have ultimate responsibility and accountability for maintaining the technology portfolio of the entire corporation, analogous to the accountability of the chief financial officer for corporate financial assets. The relationship between the VP of technology and the VP of planning is crucial to the development of an integrated planning process. They must set the standard of communication for the rest of the organization.

RESPONSIBILITIES OF THE CHIEF TECHNOLOGY OFFICER

The chief technology officer (CTO) through his or her staff must accomplish the following objectives:

- Ensure development and execution of an integrated business/technology plan for each business unit
- Tailor each technology organization and its human resources for maximum effectiveness in support of its business objectives
- Develop and administer the technology budget
- Maintain a technology overview role to exploit synergies and react to external developments

Each of these objectives will have both tactical and strategic components and will consist of the following tasks:

1. Ensure development and execution of an integrated business/technology plan for each business unit
    - Understand the strategic importance of each business unit
    - Work with corporate planning and business unit personnel to develop a technology plan concurrent with the business plan
    - Develop a technology blueprint of the entire organization that addresses expected results, risks, and probabilities of success

2. Tailor each technology organization and its human resources for maximum effectiveness
    - Create an environment and expectations, as well as assurances, for effective technology/business communication.
    - Optimize utilization of technical and human resources throughout the organization
    - Define centralized vs. divisionalized functions
    - Develop a skill inventory
    - Provide professional development to expand/refine skills
    - Implement technical recruiting to maintain experience and requisite diversity
    - Review and approve appraisals/progressions/promotions
    - Minimize disruptions from economic cycles

3. Develop and administer the technology budget
    - Plan and review with top management the company's technology portfolio and budgets
    - Spell out resources required, what and why
    - Develop effectiveness criteria and monitor programs
    - Prepare present and projected budgets
    - Gain senior management concurrence on expenditures vs. expectations

4. Maintain a technology overview role to exploit synergies and react to external developments
    - Provide feedback to business units on technology issues
    - Use forecasting and other resources to provide direction for technology development
    - Work with each segment in developing technology forecasts for each business segment

It is apparent that the chief technology officer and his staff will require a unique set of skills and talents, including: 1) business (financial, planning, and sales/marketing); 2) technology (research, development, and manufacturing); and 3) human resources (organizational effectiveness and personal development).

The correct staffing of the CTO function and its level of authority compared with the rest of the corporate management team and particularly its access to the CEO are critical to reaping the full benefits of an integrated business/technology plan.

However, another major requirement for success is to minimize bureaucracy. A lean, effective, action-oriented organization is absolutely necessary to avoid stifling both business and technology with the paperwork associated with another management layer.

In the absence of a CTO function, each business unit is left on its own to the previously mentioned requirements. This can lead to: 1) inconsistency of technology effort; 2) no synergistic effects; 3) lack of means of assessing technology effort vis-a-vis business; 4) force-fit of skills and talents into projects; 5) little top management control over technology direction apart from budget; and 6) internal politics. The overall result is a loss of technology's productivity and effectiveness.

The task of integrating technology and business is a "top down" and "bottom up" process, very similar to the process of strategic business planning. "Top down" process calls for recognizing the value of strategic planning for the management of technology and a means to convey its importance throughout the organization. The implementation requires a strong, talented corporate technology function, which assures that technology is being properly managed at multifacet corporate levels and culminates in preparing a technology portfolio, comprehensible by both business and technology functions.

The "bottom up" process calls for emphasizing and implementing technology planning at all levels and integrating it with different strategic business units (SBUs), sectors, and corporate level. It is the responsibility of the CTO to assure that functions like technology forecasting, which require specialized skills and talents and can be used throughout the corporation, are provided to guide the R&D programs. Most of the time, it is not cost effective for each SBU or sector to have its own technology forecasting function, yet any attempt to carry out technology forecasting without the involvement of various business units is likely to fail. Initially, it is an educational process where both business and technology functions must recognize the importance of technology forecasting, its evaluation, and integration with the business plans. Moreover, it is a corporate responsibility to provide the means for education and implementation.

STRATEGIC PLANNING AND MANAGEMENT OF TECHNOLOGY

Based on the experience of Alan L. Frohman,[1] the existing status of integrating technology and business strategy falls into five categories. Most of the time these categories are not easily distinguishable and in diversified industrial corporations, more than one of these categories are being practiced simultaneously without top management's awareness. The five categories are:

1. leap of faith
2. lack of faith
3. technology driven
4. market driven
5. strategic management

Leap of Faith

In this category, top management appropriates technology funds based on percent of sales or some other arbitrary criteria without understanding the reasons for that investment. Unlike other investments, eg, capital expenditure for new equipment or a new production facility, management does not pay close attention to the optimum utilization of technology resources for enhancing the business's competitive position. "The money is spent more or less on blind faith with little or no meaningful questioning." (p.21)[1] In such cases, technology plans are non-existent; most of the planning is done as the projects move along. There is also minimal interaction between market forces and technology development. Frequently, this type of budgeting is observed in emerging technologies or perceived areas of growth. In these cases, the expectations and expenditures are far in excess of what can realistically be accomplished. The problem with this kind of technology management is the impact of economic downturns, due either to recession or changes in industry structure, which adversely impact profits and consequently result in loss of faith.[1] This was exemplified by the demise of central research organizations in the 1960s.

Lack of Faith

In the lack of faith category, "business management closely controls not only the money allocated to R&D, but also how it is spent. In an extreme case, business managers involve themselves in the day-to-day management of R&D projects. The actual link in this case is that the same person overseeing the allocation of technical resources is also the one responsible for development of the business strategy. This type of link closely ties the business goals and the deployment of technical assets;" (p.21)[1] however, it too often leads to a concentration on short term projects with more visible results. Strong pressure is put on a business manager to solve current problems; this leaves little of the technical resources available for long term projects. This type of technology management is often practiced within mature industries, making them the declining industries of tomorrow.

Technology Driven

This type of management is usually found in companies dominated by scientists and engineers. The business strategy is dependent upon scientific discovery or technical breakthrough. Examples are the development of integrated circuits and advances in computer technology of the early 1980s. The result is fast progress in the field of technology-based businesses but ultimate failure as the business grows due to lack of business planning and integration with technology. In fact, the woes of Wang Corporation are a classic example of the results of such a management approach. (p.21)[1]

Customer Driven

Customer driven management is observed in companies dominated by the marketing department. The focus is to satisfy short-term needs of the customer rather than deploying technology resources for both short- and long-term needs. The functions emphasized are sales service and technical support to the existing customers, with inadequate attention being paid to the value added component of these support functions.

The impact of emerging technologies or substitution products that might affect existing markets is normally ignored and when this happens, a customer's loyalty to suppliers who only supported short-term needs often vanishes. This loss of loyalty leads to declining sales and an obsolete technology organization. (p.21)[1]

Strategic Management

Strategic management of technology takes into consideration existing and anticipated business needs, which have been developed through the process of strategic business planning, and formulates a technology strategy. The business and technology strategies are then evaluated to determine their practicality in supporting short- and long-term business objectives, existing vs required resources, skills/talents, and the competence of both business and technology organizations. This task is accomplished by asking and answering a series of questions, as listed by Domenic Bitondo and Alan Frohman[2]. They can be broken down into the following seven categories.

Technology Objectives

- "Is it our objective to apply technology for product innovation; for process innovation; for product performance improvement; for cost reduction?
- "Do we need to replenish our technology (ie, advance and/or catch-up with the state-of-art)?

Technology Selection

- "What technology(ies) do we need to invest in for current products?
- "What future technology(ies) do we need to invest in to provide opportunities for future growth?
- "Should we exploit existing technological capability for maximum return and/or new products for new markets?

Technology Investment Level

- "How much should we invest in each technology?
- "How stable should our investment level be to maintain R&D investment?

External Intelligence

- "How much effort do we expend obtaining knowledge of competitive and external direction?
- "How do we organize the technological surveillance effort?

Technological Posture

- "How close to the state-of-the-art should the firm's technology be? Should we be the leader? Or just maintain an awareness?

- "What should the balance be between basic approach, applied approach, development and applications engineering?

Technology Acquisition

- "To what extent should internal versus external sources of technology be relied on? Licensing, joint venture, acquisition, other divisions, central research organization, contract research (government and outside companies), and internal development are possible options.

Technology Organization and Policies

- "How do we organize technology in the business (eg, centralized versus decentralized)?
- "Should a project, functional or matrix organization be used?
- "Is a "dual ladder" necessary?
- "Should R&D facilities be established in other countries?
- "Are the hiring and reward practices consistent with the strategy?" (p.22)[2] *Reprinted with permission.*

In the process of asking and evaluating these questions, it is extremely important to separate perceived or biased opinions as much as possible. One way of doing this is to analyze and evaluate past performance attributes of the technology organization. It is assumed that business functions have gone through the same rigorous analysis in the strategic business planning methodology.

Five Steps of Integrating Technology

A number of techniques have been developed for integrating technology and strategic business planning process that employ the synergistic effects of portfolio planning techniques. Emergence of these techniques was initiated by the realization that portfolio planning methods by themselves do not address technology issues. Techniques analogous to portfolio planning must be developed to bridge the gap between strategic business planning and technology. Most of these techniques were developed by consulting companies in the 1980s, and some have been published in literature.[2-5]

Each one of these approaches consist of some or all of the following five steps:

1. Identification and definition of a company's technologies which are given the name, "Strategic Technology Areas" or "Technology Planning Units" (analogous to strategic busi-

ness units) and preparation of a list of candidates for technology investments.
2. Establishment of business criteria and constraints and
    screening the list of candidates (equivalent to industry at-
    tractiveness and business strength).
3. Identification of risks and rewards.
4. Graphic display of technology portfolio.
5. Selection and resource allocation for technology develop-
    ment.

Development of the above five tasks requires the involvement of
the R&D staff, consultants, senior scientists, marketing staff, and production staff plus a final review with the President and CEO of the
corporation. The role of these functions varies depending upon the
magnitude of resource allocation and importance of technology to
the long term viability of the corporation.

There is a clear distinction between the approach developed by
Stacey and other techniques. Stacey's approach is based on using
technology forecasting as a means of integrating technology and business planning; the other techniques, although clearly emphasizing
the importance of marketing and other functions in developing a
technology portfolio, do not provide a mechanism to identify areas of
technology importance to various businesses. The five steps of integrating technology and business are illustrated using Stacey's approach. (pp.18–20)[4]

Step 1 - Identification and Definition of Technologies and Candidates

The first step, defining strategic technology areas, consists of a
technology audit in which the company reviews and defines its own
products and processes to determine which technologies are employed in each. These technologies are then compared and evaluated
based on existing and projected state of the art. This evaluation results in the identification of focused and exploratory R&D projects.
Focused R&D is essentially related to existing and key technologies
used in the company's processes and products, whereas exploratory
R&D is more conceptual and is used in identifying, evaluating, and
developing emerging technologies pertinent to existing products
and processes or in the development of new products.

The various inputs involved in the identification of focused R&D
include the evaluation of a product line in its entirety (as described
in Chapter 8), which can be summarized as examining existing products and processes, monitoring and evaluating competitor's products

and processes, and monitoring different market segments for changing customer needs. Any substitution products or emerging technologies which can impact the customers is also an integral part of this evaluation. Such an evaluation identifies all areas of R&D work that are likely to impact a product line.

Exploratory or conceptual R&D projects are an outcome of monitoring the existing technology and business environment, plus new idea generation based on the market needs of businesses in which the company participates or wishes to participate.

This step provides a list of all R&D candidates, irrespective of their profit potential.

Step 2 - Establishment of Business Criteria and Constraints and Screening of Candidates

This screening consists of both macro and micro factors. At the macro level, they relate to broad external events such as sociological, political, economic and technological indicators at both national and international levels. At the micro level, the concerns are about key and emerging technologies that might impact the industry, markets, products, processes, and/or competition. This evaluation acts as a broad screen for rejecting the areas of work with obvious major drawbacks.

Step 3 - Identification of Risks and Rewards of Selected Candidates

This step evaluates both business and technology risks and rewards such as profit potential, investment costs, impact of technology failure on businesses, time to commercialize, and probability of success. These factors are then used to develop a risk-evaluation matrix as shown in Figure 10.1.

The risk/reward criteria in the figure represents a hypothetical example of R&D options obtained from the technological forecasts. For example, candidate A has a high profit potential, high investment cost, short time for commercialization and a low risk of failure that is typically the case in key technologies. Based on this evaluation, a company with a low cash position may decide to form a joint venture and, thus, exploit its technological strength to participate in an attractive business.[4]

The risk/reward criteria of different R&D candidates can be quantified by assigning them relative numerical values for comparative purposes. The screening process can be used for both new and existing

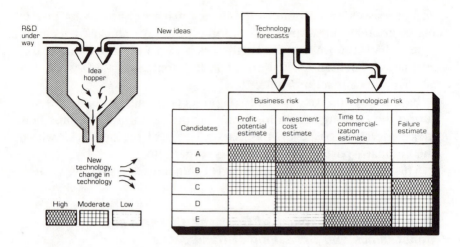

Figure 10.1   The Use of Technology Forecasts to Locate R&D Options in a Risk Evaluation[4] *Reprinted with permission.*

R&D programs. Completing such an evaluation challenges R&D organizations to think beyond existing programs and may result in abandoning existing programs in favor of new ones.

Step 4 - Preparation of Tech-Risk Array

Figure 10.1 indicates the technological and business judgments on the various R&D programs. The Tech-Risk Array then fits these alternatives into a matrix which portrays relative business and technological risks for the company. To formulate this matrix, R&D programs are divided into two major categories: focused R&D and exploratory R&D.

Each one of these categories has sub components. "For example, focused R&D includes: 1) existing technologies; 2) changed technologies resulting from changes in engineering developments, competition or markets; and 3) key technologies (technologies either newly in use or at the verge of commercialization). Exploratory R&D deals with technologies that are at various stages of development and are far from being commercially viable, such as: 1) emerging technologies; 2) conceptual technologies; and 3) unknown technologies." (p.19)[4]

Since the end result of technologies is either a product or process, the R&D ideas are further classified by categories of business application such as: 1) improvement to current products or processes; 2) replacement of current products or processes; and 3) creation of new products or processes.

A matrix illustrating the technologies and their impact on business applications is shown in Figure 10.2. Alternative technologies are presented on the vertical axis with the technological risk, in terms of successful development and commercialization, increasing from top to bottom. The horizontal axis represents alternative uses of technology in processes and products with the business risk, in terms of payoff and uncertainty, increasing from left to right. For example, improvements in products and process using proven technologies involve the least business risk, but the magnitude of the risk increases as replacement or new products and processes are introduced. The magnitude of risk also increases when new technologies are introduced in existing products and processes. The highest risk business activity is when new technologies are used for new processes and products.[4]

Technology forecasting techniques provide a means to examine the list of options and assign them a place in a Tech-Risk Array. For example, the R&D candidates *A* through *E* from the risk valuations in Figure 10.1 would be positioned as shown in Figure 10.3. The development of this figure is illustrated by considering candidate A in Figure 10.1. It is classified in Step 3 as a new product, hence a high business risk but uses an existing technology resulting in low technological risk. Whereas, candidate *E* is the reverse of *A,* the technology risk is high but the business risk is low.

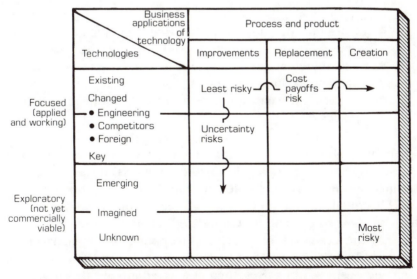

Figure 10.2 Array of Technologies and R&D Options[4]
Reprinted with permission.

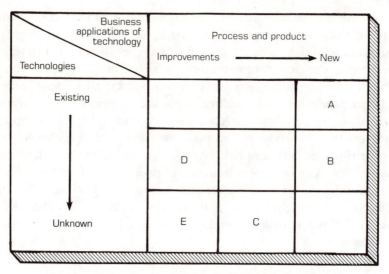

Figure 10.3   Tech-Risk Array of R&D Options[4]
Reprinted with permission.

Step 5 - Evaluation, Selection, and Resource Allocation for Technologies and R&D Options

This step is based on the overall business objectives of the corporation. During the selection process, a variety of strategic questions are asked, such as:

- Does the company wish to participate in the internal development of new businesses? And, if so, at what risk level?
- Are sufficient resources allocated to maintaining and enhancing existing businesses?
- Is the right balance between product and process R&D in place?

The portfolio display in Figure 10.3 helps in addressing the above questions by utilizing a graphic illustration of R&D projects and their business potential. For example, the majority of the technologies and R&D candidates present either a high technology risk (*C* and *E*) or high business risk (*A* and *B*). Candidate *D* offers a moderate risk level but has the drawback of a low profit opportunity. If management does not like the portfolio of technologies, as representative of the strategic business objectives, then new programs are developed and evaluated to meet the corporate objectives.

Of course, in the actual business environment, many more facets of technological and business risks are likely to be included in the analysis and result in a more detailed Tech-Risk Array.[4]

CONCLUDING REMARKS

It must be recognized that the development of a technology portfolio addresses only one aspect of the strategic management of technology by providing a mechanism of integrating and evaluating technology/business objectives. Some of the other important aspects of strategic technology management which are not addressed in technology portfolio planning are:

- Exploiting synergistic effects of different technologies.
- Optimum utilization of resources which entails hiring, training, and developing the right skills and talents ahead of the needs.
- Maintaining the calibre and competencies of technology management.
- Developing effectiveness criteria.
- Providing an environment of work where creativity and innovation are recognized.

The above issues, along with technology portfolio management, must be addressed in their entirety in the effective strategic management of technology, and both must have the recognition and support of top corporate management.

In summary, strategic management of technology takes into consideration short- and long-term corporate objectives and translates them into an action plan. The planning process is carried out in concert with strategic business planning and considers the needs and constraints of both business and technology. Strategic planning of business and technology have many similarities and differences, which if not understood, will result in their being out of phase. A major part of this process is recognition and consideration of the differences in the management of technology and technologists as compared to business and businessmen. These differences occur due to a number of diverse characteristics between scientists/technologists and businessmen, such as educational background, personality traits, and inherent needs of self-satisfaction. The organization as an operator can recognize and accommodate these diverse individuals by encouraging and providing cross-functional training, formulating a mechanism that enhances team spirit, and emphasizing the importance of both technology and business functions as being essential for success in the global competitive environment of today. Organizations that tend to make one function subservient to another, such as technology to business or vice-versa, are not likely to obtain optimal results from technology, and strategic business/technology planning will only be of limited use and become more a means of operational control rather than strategic management.

A properly planned technology effort takes into consideration the optimum distribution and use of resources, the right mix of skills and talents and develops a technology portfolio and set of effectiveness criteria.

It is obvious that such an effort is time consuming and requires specialized talents; therefore, unless demanded and supported by top management, it will never be accomplished. The consequences of not doing so are the inefficient use of resources, loss of opportunities and competitive position, and a host of other failures, which manifest as:

- new processes not being effectively competitive because of cost curve position of markets served.
- existing technologies falling behind state of the art and impacting the cost/price/performance of product lines.
- cost reduction and capacity expansion programs failing to deliver competitive advantage.
- major snags occurring in the development and commercialization of new products.
- safety and environmental issues becoming a major concern.

One or more of the above factors have been responsible for the loss of competitive position in a number of corporations, resulting in their restructuring through divestitures, acquisitions, and massive layoffs. These actions were taken by corporations to stay competitive, but they do not address their long-term viability. The latter is a strong function of developing and deploying technological strengths to satisfy socio-economic needs. The overall purpose of this book has been to provide a rational approach for integrating technology and business that, when combined together, will result in a strong competitive force for existing and new businesses.

REFERENCES

1. Frohman, A.L.: Managing the company's technology assets. *Research Management,* 23:20-24, 1980.

2. Bitondo, D., Frohman, A.L.: Linking technology and business planning. *Research Management,* 24:22, 1981.

3. Ketteringham, J.M.: Technology's Role in the Renewal Process, Arthur D. Little, Special Report, October 1983/R831001, pp. 26-46.

4. Stacey, G.S.: Technology Forecasting and Tech-Risk Array *Battelle Inputs to Planning/Review No. 14,* Battelle Memorial Institute, Columbus, Ohio, 1984.

5. Fusfeld, A.R.: Strategic Management of R&D, Rensselar Polytechnic Institute, 1985.

INDEX

Bold print indicates illustration